'There is a spark of magic inside everyone. The tragedy of life is most people never realise their true potential, they live and die without ever turning that spark into a flame. Find your magic spark. It will turn your life into an unforgettable adventure, a bright, eternal flame that will live on much longer than you do. Live your life and set the world on fire.'

To see the light, you have to experience the darkness.

What they are saying about Motivation from a Tortured Mind

"I have been personally developing for 12 years now. Michael's book MFATM has certainly challenged me to become more. The insights and hard hitting points will leave you inspired and motivated to do exactly that - 'Become More'. One of the best reads in my life."

Craig White - Successful Entrepreneur, Author and Leadership & Success Coach

"From the moment I picked up this book, it grabbed me. It is one of the most exhilarating, emotional rollercoaster rides I have ever been on, and I loved every minute of it.

If you are facing your own challenges & adversity in life then Michael and this book will show you by applying simple principles, you can and will change your life."

Sylvia Laing
Wife, Mum & Successful Business Woman

"'Motivation From a Tortured Mind' is a scintillating read. Michael Khatkar writes in a very unique style.

Once you open the cover the book is very hard to put down. And if you do, you cannot wait to pick it up again & carry on reading.

The unique writing style of Michael Khatkar puts this book shoulder to shoulder with 'the greats' such as Jim Rohn, Zig Ziglar & Tony Robbins.

The chapters on goal setting and 'your song' are amongst the best ever written in the personal development genre.

Michael Khatkar's first book, 'Motivation From a Tortured Mind' is a compelling read that will undoubtedly go on to be a best seller. We cannot recommend it highly enough."

Silver Premier Executive Distributors, Leaders, Entrepeneurs Mike & Amanda Bibby, Kleeneze.

"I had no idea when I picked up this book the power that was held within its pages. Michael eloquently shares with you an honest account of his deepest darkest thoughts. Using an unconventional approach, he inspires and motivates the readers to take a good look at their own life. This book truly has the ability to motivate, inspire and effect changes in other human beings like no other book I have ever read.

Chapter 9 "Any goal, lifetime ambition or target will drive a stake of desire right through your heart, if it is fuelled and powered by YOUR SONG"

This chapter alone makes you re-evaluate the whole concept of goal setting and helps you understand what is needed for you to achieve the success YOU ultimately DESIRE."

Debra Gee - Network Marketing Entrepreneur

About The Author

Fascinated by the incredible power and fortitude of the human psyche, throughout the entirety of my life and career, I've studied people in one way or another from the analysis and hypothesis of Human Psychology & Behaviour to the indisputable, tangible lives of real people. Through this intrinsic, perennial learning I've carved a successful career in people orientated industries and continue to comprehend the fundamental ingredients and perception of success & failure.

My personal journey frequently riddled with provocation, controversy and often acute subjectivity has only just begun, destinations are rarely reached with curiosity and imagination harmoniously, opening new doors and bulldozing conventional, humdrum walls.

I sincerely hope 'Motivation from a Tortured Mind' incites and arouses your spectacular mind and manages to instigate even a miniscule positive change in your perception, attitude and belief, widening your vision and bringing into sharp focus the destination you crave.

'It's the shining, lighthouse beacon that relentlessly lights the path to your personal utopia, your promised land your infinite wishes and fantasies. It's your incessant blinding light at the end of the tunnel.'

Motivation
from a
Tortured Mind

MICHAEL KHATKAR

Filament
Publishing

First published in 2013 by

Filament Publishing Ltd
16 Croydon Road,
Waddon,
Croydon,
Surrey CR0 4PA
Tel: 020 8688 2598
info@filamentpublishing.com
www.filamentpublishing.com

Design and layout by ALS Designs, Waterlooville, Hampshire.
www.als-designs.co.uk

Printed in the UK by Berforts Information Press.

ISBN 978-1-908691-44-6

Motivation from a Tortured Mind is dedicated to

Mum, Dad and Kieran.

And every single person that has believed in me and particularly all those that haven't – The inspiration from you all, has been equally powerful and relevant.

Contents

Michael Khatkar

Introduction

'There is a spark of magic inside everyone. The tragedy of life is most people never realise their true potential, they live and die without ever turning that spark into a flame. Find your magic spark. It will turn your life into an unforgettable adventure, a bright, eternal flame that will live on much longer than you do. Live your life and set the world on fire.'

I haven't climbed Mount Everest. I'm not a billionaire. I'm not a celebrity. I'm not even an ex-convict. I've had all the rollercoaster successes and failures that many people encounter. I've learnt that almost everything we experience, every corner we turn, every emotional embroilment has an intriguing story to tell and will be meaningful in a multitude of ways to an entire spectrum of people. Everyone has within them their own book of tales, inspiration and adventures that undoubtedly will motivate and enlighten others.

The precise moment we appear from the womb, an audacious plot begins to antagonise and counteract the miraculous life we're consecrated with, from that first breath of air, the forces of nature, our circumstances and the environment conceptualise our demise and endeavour to return us back to where we originated from. Every day of blessed life is a fight for our right to have a place in this world.

The unpredictability of our unavailing lives is inane and frivolous, with the grim reaper only ever one step behind us. Your greatest challenge is to live the life you dream of, before his deathly scythe decapitates your peripheral existence.

'Motivation from a Tortured Mind' explores the wounding depths of human cataclysms to staggering inspirational revelations of hope, vision and possibility and yet both definitive extremes of the scale lead to epic renunciations of living a sub-standard, second best life. Learning derived from conventional milestones to the preposterously grotesque and bizarre, it is an incomparable approach to the provocation and encouragement of the human psyche and the quintessence of life itself.

CHAPTER 1

Curiosity

Life can be easily lived in a diminutive puddle or travelled on a vast ocean of discovery but until you gaze upon that sea of hope, vision and possibility, exploring, determining and pressing every button that enforces aspiration and action, you'll be unlikely to experience its symbolic drenching of success.'

The Hospital

They all had tears in their puffy over-cried eyes, almost caustic bitter tracks down their faces where the tears had meandered and left their sad mark. Their expressions were a bizarre mixture of melancholy and strained joy, for some reason I thought they were all holding hands too.

These were all faces very familiar to me, comforting faces I'd known all my life. They were staring through handkerchief sized panes of glass, just enough to fit a face into. The panes of glass were about five to six foot from the floor of the magnolia painted wall and made the five people staring in all appear to be the same height. I couldn't focus on anything else except stare at the people framed in the panes of glass, all smiling and now waving too. Were they gesturing a welcome or a goodbye, I hoped it was a welcome, I couldn't ever imagine a farewell with these particular people, I loved them dearly.

There wasn't much else going on in the dream, except for reasons unbeknown to me I was in a hospital bed. I'd worked that out from the childhood memories of being in hospital, the clinical smell and the hanging white light globes, images and aromas that always meant being away from my loving family, not to mention the prospect of some ghastly medical procedure to look forward to. At least on this occasion my mother & father, two older brothers and my aunty were here with me, albeit parted by the obligatory magnolia hospital wall. It didn't feel melancholy, like it used to. After all it was only a dream. My visitors seemed very pleased to see me and of course in a moment I knew I'd wake up in my own bed, in a home that was always filled with feelings of happiness, love, childhood contentment and my Dad's speciality the best full cooked breakfasts in the world. With the thought of eggs, beans & sausages I smiled back at the five wonderful faces and once again mused at the fact they all seemed the same height, when in reality they were all differing sizes, my mother at 5' 4", my father at 5' 6", my brothers both at around 5' 10" and the tallest of the lot, my aunty at 5' 11". Through the panes of glass they were all 5' 6".

Right it was time to wake. Now I could always do that with fluid ease. In any dream or nightmare I had the wonderful knack, not sure how and maybe it's one everyone has, of just closing my eyes, thinking of waking in my bed and hey presto, it would work every time, regardless of what shenanigans were going on in my dream. I'd escaped all sorts of situations, including demons, school teachers (note at the time these were classified in the same category as Demons), bullies and even at that age of fourteen, immense responsibilities (which I seemed to have shirked for one reason or another for most of my younger life). In most cases I'd caused a troublesome state of affairs that I needed to circumvent from. This one wasn't troublesome, just a bit offbeat, particularly as I was now starting to feel awkward, above all because I couldn't really move much, the hospital bed, with its familiar hospital bed smell, seemed quite confining, I could sense myself getting agitated and I had a strange paranoid premonition that something detestable was about to happen.

I closed my eyes and that beautiful rush of cognition swept over me as I was being transported back to my own bed, a mixture of anticipation of home, a full cooked breakfast and sheer relief as I'd just had deliverance from whatever was going to happen in hospital.

Think about a time when your contemplation of a forthcoming event is grossly outweighed by the reality of what actually happens.

You're at a firework display. It's been a wonderful evening, full of colour, wonder & surprise. Now its time for the final act, the magnanimous explosive masterpiece that will herald the close of the evening. You're told the firework that's about to be lit will light up the sky with a thousand different colours, have deafening cannon booms and gloriously sparkle for at least 20 minutes, oh and you should stand well back, at least 25 metres, as this spectacular gunpowder extravaganza could be quite dangerous. This fiery little monster will leave you exhilarated beyond belief and will be an awesome finale to what has already been a stunning evening of fire, light & total pyrotechnical entertainment. Your anticipation is beyond belief. Your mind has conjured up its own reality of the forthcoming event, based on what's already happened during the evening, your previous memories, the excitement, chatter & expectations of the people around you and most importantly, your unique human ability of IMAGINATION.

The person lighting it, edges slowly towards the monumental monolith buried 6 inches into the ground. Its standing firm with fifteen thick inches proudly displayed ready to impress with the show it has inside, just waiting to explode as soon as it mixes with the tiniest of sparks. He stretches out his arm, teases the audience with a countdown 5...4...3...2...1 and finally lights the blue touch paper. The fuse is twenty inches long and blindingly glows as it burns towards the twelve inch girth of the firework. It almost goads the crowd, it fizzes enthusiastically, its almost shouting out at you 'wait for it, wait for it, wait for it, I'm coming, just wait for it!!' In your mind you hear the theme to 'Mission Impossible'. You start to wonder what could happen if its faulty and explodes in the wrong direction, you consider carnage of 3rd degree burns, sirens and an A & E ward that can't cope with the casualties. You even contemplate losing an eye thanks to a multi-coloured fireball that rockets uncontrollably straight into your face. Your irrational thoughts encourage you to step even further back, however the anticipation is tingling and awe inspiring. This has now become the foreplay of an almighty, intense, torrid, jazzy climax just waiting to happen. There are people already covering their ears. Kids have retreated deeper into the crowd with scared apprehension. Finally, the dazzling fuse disappears into the big, torpedo of a firework. We're now at the point of no return, not even a bucket of cold water poured over it can stop the build up it was engineered for... And then... NOTHING!!! Of course have patience, it's just setting off the reaction inside, in a few seconds it'll burst into life... Here we go... and NOTHING!!

How do you feel now? Deflated, dissatisfied, cheated, disillusioned and above all disappointed. Now, that's the feeling of an anti-climax, a slump in your emotions, a miserable unfulfilled, let-down. I know there are many times you've had this petulant and sour, negative feeling and undoubtedly many more to come.

Now, let's go back to my unnerving childhood hospital dream.

I'm just about to wake from a disturbing dream, the images have now been overtaken by the blissful feeling of waking up in my own bed and forgetting the hospital smell and melancholy faces of the people I cherish.

Total disaster strikes, I've just witnessed the 'firework failure syndrome', expectations dashed, heart sunk and a tremendous downturn in my emotional state. I was still in hospital, same faces staring at me, same clinical smells and the very same constricting bed. It didn't need a second try to wake up, I'd just had the horrific realisation I was awake and this was my gloomy reality.

The harshness of my bizarre & unlikely situation was now compounded by a searing pain from my stomach, an excruciating detail that I hadn't noticed when I initially woke. There was a tube caustically piercing my arm, its point of entry covered with plasters, its other end attached to a plastic bag full of clear liquid. There was a big silver machine with buttons, agitated dials and a persistent, penetrating beep. Even all that confusing peculiarity was insignificant compared to the sharp, bludgeoning pain coming from my head and the inability to establish how I materialised in this atrocious and improbable predicament. It later transpired I'd been here for two weeks.

Suffice to say it had been a mysterious fatal condition, I'd been saved from near-death, predominantly by the rapid action of the ambulance crew, their defibrillator and amazing expertise in keeping patients alive, especially when they were unsure what had caused such a sudden physical collapse.

Was this my epiphany, my new beginning, that turning point so many entrepreneurs, celebrities and people that achieve exceptional feats of courage and endurance preach about? The cornerstone of all their success, the very reason they become so successful, the driving force that pushes them to achieving insurmountable eminence and prosperity. The foundation, the rock on which they build a boundless, undefeatable attitude, a laser like focus and a vision that can see further and beyond average, mere mortals.

Hardly, otherwise I'd have that overwhelming success, the impregnable attitude, the invincible focus and a vision that locks onto the future and flies me effortlessly to my desired destination. I'd possess all the elegant grandeur, palatial riches & ritzy opulence scarcely associated with mediocrity. Not to mention shelves of accolades, demonstrating my enduring performance, my distinctions and deeds almost impervious and unavailable to most of humanity.

It may not have signalled my rebirth, or even heralded a corner-turning resolution but even at the impressionable age of fourteen, the dreadful experience taught me some intrinsic lessons. Lessons, that left an indelible legacy throughout my life.

The Button

Pristine, preening and unquestionably looking and feeling a million dollars, I confidently strutted onto the deck of the glorious yacht. Draped in white, the sun was beaming, the heat was searing and my neat linen trousers bellowed in the wind like the enormous sails of the vessel. The swagger was of a well dressed confident man, the elation only exacerbated by the knowledge of staring eyes. Oh yes, I was most certainly turning heads, probably more because of the blinding white glare of my clothes than any other reason but that didn't matter. I was attracting attention and not entirely for the wrong reasons. I must have looked like a famous Indian film-star, not necessarily one of the cute handsome ones but at least one of the swarthy, philandering villains, either way I appreciated people rubbernecking to see the unlikely, lady-killer spectacle in white. My million dollar swagger was interrupted by something glistening in the shine of the sun that sparkled and caught my eye.

A shining silver spherical button slightly larger than the size of a tennis ball on the wall, five foot from the ground, its lustrous finish was almost blinding as my white outfit. Etched across the button in capital letters the word 'PUSH' and without any hesitation whatsoever, without any consideration of the potential consequences and within the gaze of the ogling crowd, I stretched out my arm and with the palm of my hand smacked the sun-warmed button and with a loud thud, pushed it hard. Whatever reason the glaring crowd were watching and scrutinising me, they were glad they were, what happened next would have been an unforgettable moment, a story which years on they still regale with great glee to their friends.

What I was totally oblivious to was the equally glistening and shiny shower faucet approximately three foot above the button. Upon pushing the button, the faucet forcibly sprayed out gallons of freezing cold water, which consequently turned my impeccable presentation to that of a drenched rat, a very wet, shocked and embarrassed Indian film-star, a soaking lothario with a hugely dampened ego, a comedy moment made even funnier by the unlikely girly shriek I let out as the freezing water doused me. The situation was clearly so amusing it not only caused raucous laughter but also a round of rapturous applause.

Curiosity, an intense desire to know, an emotion related to natural inquisitive behaviour, such as exploration, investigation and learning. Our deep-seated desire to learn and experience, theoretically It's the opposite of the 'what if syndrome'.

Traditionally the 'what-if syndrome' is based around our negative emotions, the negativity of worry, we spend almost our entire lives worrying about something or other; What if this happened, what if that happened, what if he says no, what if she says yes, what if I lose my job, what if I have a car accident, what if my television blows up, what if the world ends, what if, what if, what if. This is how we spend our days, worrying about absolutely anything there is to worry about. Practically all of our 'what if', questions avidly revolve around the detrimental, pessimistic and counterproductive facets of our existence. My personal 'what if syndrome' has been largely based on 'what if I don't do this, do that, touch this, touch that, say this say that. How will I ever know the outcome, unless I take the action to actually find out. If I don't take the necessary action and I never find out, how can I possibly live with myself, it'll constantly plague my mind that an untold story or experience that could have been mine now unsatisfactorily eludes me, I should have just done it, now I'll never know or understand what could have happened. That curious, inquisitive and meddlesome mind of mine has caused me reams of untold anguish as well as acres of valuable learning.

There are times when one just has to press the allegorical button, irrespective of what the outcome may be, of course there are times when it'll be regretful but there will also be times when it's the best possible thing you could have done. Taking those somewhat precarious chances elude from locating your own personal buttons, that when metaphorically pressed, present the life you truly want, entwined with the emotions that catalyse it into action.

Post-Mortem

The 'slab' patiently awaits us. A pristine worktop of cold, deathly white ceramic, in a brightly lit room, surrounded by ashen grey floors, white tiles and dulled stainless steel with the clinically pungent aroma of disinfectant and astringent floor cleaner. Subdued, vacuous and uninteresting aside from the malevolence of the brushed metallic trolley, a wheeled haven for evil implements capable of slicing through dead flesh, prodding, piercing and impaling diseased organs and unsympathetically crushing bones and cracking skulls open.

For most of us the only day we are unconditionally comfortable in the bare skin we're born with and brazenly, without a second of hesitation, nakedly splay ourselves under the gaze of strangers, is the one day when we're least concerned with our wrinkles, unforgiving fat and misshapen bodies. All our commercial and human indebtedness, our idiosyncrasies and behaviours may not be forgiven but are forced to be forgotten as the emotionless coroner prepares to scythe through our rigid blood-frozen, pallid dead skin on a journey of medical unearthing.

The shining blades of contrived bodily destruction and tissue separation are razor sharp and eager as is the expertly precise hand that swerves them through rigor mortised muscle membranes. Forty eight hours earlier this would have been heinous blood-soaked murder of the most macabre kind, now it's a valuable, albeit still macabre, profession that determines the very reasons of death. The facial expression sullen but peaceful as the merciless knife incises through the leathery anaemic skin, a trickle of bitter dead blood dares to appear, once rampaging through the body giving life, now with cells destroyed, meaningless, void of oxygen and barely recognisable in its deathly deep, reddish brown hue, the giver of life is now a coroners inconvenience and unnecessary mess.

Collar bone to navel the deep laceration bears little blood but with two stainless steel forceps is drawn open like a set of flesh curtains, tearing akin to removing chicken skin from the pink breast meat. Butcher shop pungency and a set of already diseasing organs that were abruptly halted in their operation for reasons yet to be determined, sit there in their anatomically correct positions. A once beating heart, sickly yellow spleen, bile filled stomach and a convoluted colon harbouring the last supper all now under scrutiny of signs where life decided to cease.

The cause and precise time of death will soon become apparent, the tell-tale signs of which organ gave up the fight for life will be screaming out as it is barbarously carved open. However, the impossibility is determining when the person actually stopped living not when the physical body ceased to function. There is a distinct time lapse between dying and not living the life that is possible. Therefore no Coroners inquisition into the cause of death can ascertain what percentage of life was actually lived before the calamity of death became reality.

Irrespective of where the long or short goodbye to physical life began, the human heart is ordered to cease pumping the bloody electricity that manufactures the existence of every living human-being. The provider of life itself is empowered, sanctioned and controlled by the grey matter within our brains.

With a medical tool that can only be described as a crazed spinning circular saw, the Coroner dissects the rib cage and with a sickening crunch of bone, using his latex glove covered hands, cracks open the rib-cage. The once protective shield now helplessly in two pieces and displaying the uncovered dead heart, no bigger than a clenched fist and no more than an oddly shaped mass of fibrous fatty tissue. Once, this heart was capable of so much, now without the rib-cage so vulnerable, lifeless and absolutely pointless.

Four valves that pump the life-blood around the body, ensuring vital oxygen is carried via the red blood cells essential for every human organ to function and stay alive. The Coroner diligently inspects every tiny modicum of the heart and can competently distinguish between healthy, dead and diseased tissue, including verification of the time when heartbeats finally ceased and siphoned life from the body. However this expert of the dead cannot see metaphorical, symbolic buttons that every individual has within their palpitating heart.

An integral set of heartfelt buttons that only activate and begin their chain reactions when curiosity and imagination are utilised. The further curiosity is investigated using the power of imagining, the stronger the desire, vision and focus of the individual. The tragedy of the figurative buttons is most people never locate them. Therefore the strong and forceful emotions associated with the buttons are never prompted.

If the coroner, along with the diseases he locates, could physically see the set of unused buttons within the dead person and understand the time lapse between dying and not living the life possible, his report would read as follows.

Time of Physical Death: 14th August 2011

Time of unfulfilled Death: Unknown

Cause of Death: Heart Failure

Cause of unfulfilled Death: Failure to locate buttons of Desire

1. As a human button is pressed, much like the cold water I was showered with, an instant reaction occurs. This repercussion although very individual should feel like a surge of energy flowing and cascading through every blood cell, artery and vein of your body, with every tiny hair standing to attention electrified and stunned by the raw flow of emotions attached to desire. If you really understood the sheer power of pressing your own buttons surely you would leave no stone unturned in locating such a commanding impetus. A physical and mental higher state of consciousness that is legal and already resident within your beating heart.

2. Let your sense of curiosity and formidable imagination dive into the sea of the unknown because within your psyche is a dormant, lethargic monster waiting to be awoken with the impulse from pressing your buttons. Every individual has this potential and possibility. Don't leave your physical existence with un-pressed buttons, untapped potential and unrealised desire. The explorative process of using your imagination will lead to enormous success associated with pursuing those elements of desire.

Pressing your metaphorical buttons of desire, will result in a very different Coroners report:

Time of Physical Death: 14th August 2011

Time of unfulfilled Death: 14th August 2011

Cause of Death: Heart Failure

Cause of unfulfilled Death: Not Applicable

There is an immense sea of curiosity, waiting to be discovered. Set sail upon it with your life raft and witness its vastness. The magnitude of the unknown is infinitive and within it lies the difference between what you are and what you possess and all the things you aspire to. Life can be easily lived in a diminutive puddle or travelled on a vast ocean of discovery but until you gaze upon that sea of hope, vision and possibility, exploring, determining and pressing every button that enforces aspiration and action, you'll be unlikely to experience its symbolic drenching of success.

The Cheating Pharmacist

We were all beginning to lose sight of how she used to look as her appearance over the last few months had seen some dramatic changes. Physical changes that were necessary for improving her health and subsequently prolonging her life. So even though she was becoming increasingly unrecognisable, knowing that this meant she wouldn't die prematurely was the only convincing we needed. Of course, at that tender pre-teen age nothing was scarier than losing one's parents, so when Mum lost a vast amount of weight it was a sigh of relief but the beginning of another extraordinary and bizarre adventure in curiosity.

My inquiring mind was perplexed, how could something so minute have such a disproportionate effect? The tricolour capsules that Mum took twice a day, staved her hunger for days on end, hence the loss of weight. Decades ago it was as simple as that, obesity was tackled with potent appetite suppressants. Eat nothing lose weight, with absolutely no regards for the ramifications of such a harsh regime, one that naturally today would be frowned upon and certainly not available from the family doctor.

Mum wasn't the only obese person in our family, yours truly had always been on the slightly, okay not slightly but considerably chunky side of the fence. In fact maybe roly-poly, rotund, dumpy and porky were more appropriate colloquialisms, or let's just say FAT! I was fat, there was no escaping, hiding or lying about the obvious. I was substantially larger than anyone else my age and there were probably people twice my age that faded into insignificance in my young, portly larger-than-life presence. I was probably overweight because my Mother was overweight, that's not an excuse, however some eating habits are naturally adopted and learnt through our parents, as are many other habits and behaviours. Or even simpler than that, I just ate what Mum ate and probably the same quantities. Now imagine the scenario, obese Mother plus obese kid, slim Mother plus obese kid, slim Mother plus curious tricolour capsules plus obese and curious kid. I think you're getting the picture. Downright inquisitiveness and a necessity to be slim like Mother, led me to the opaque brown bottle containing the magic slimming pills. Without any hesitation whatsoever I swallowed one before going to school on one normal Wednesday morning, which went on to become an unforgettable milestone of mischief and bedlam. What a prodigious day that was! The string of events following the intake of a drug that has since been prohibited in this country was unquestionably intangible and completely surreal, particularly for an eleven year old child.

A huge internal commotion started, a quarrelsome hurricane was unleashed within my stomach, it swirled with a tumultuous annoyance, it was furious. The ensuing displeasure was unbelievably disproportionate to the fairly insignificant size of the capsule, every few minutes another fuse was lit followed by a heated explosion, almost as if there was something alive within me. The tiny drug had grown into a feisty deformed monster with meat cleavers for claws and razor blades for teeth and it was scraping and biting itself out, any minute it was going to burst out showering everyone in my vicinity with blood and guts, the rancid contents of my stomach were about to rupture my skin and split my body in two. It was the greatest gut-wrenching pain imaginable. The severity lasted no more than twenty minutes but seemed like a month of misery. Until this day I can feel the fury and eruptions it caused and yet it was self-inflicted, complete irresponsibility a total disregard for health or well-being and yet this was the ludicrous foundation of so much more to come.

Twenty minutes of uncompromising physical suffering followed by a full twelve hours of nausea accompanied by a relentless loathing of food, from the sight of it to the mere smell and even the thought of it, was enough to actually bring vomit to the back of my young throat. I was in awe, completely gob-smacked that it had that shocking affect. One tiny blue, red and yellow plastic capsule created an extraordinary twelve hour inexplicable aftermath resulting in absolutely nil-by-mouth. There was no wonder Mother had lost so much weight, these pills were more dedicated than any kind of human orientated dieting imaginable. Albeit I was perturbed by the pain my mum must have suffered with each pill consumed, I convinced myself the painful unexpected consequence must have exclusively happened in my fledgling undeveloped body, whereas adults wouldn't witness such an abhorrent side effect.

At such a young age one day without food has an immediate effect, whether it really was physical or psychological, I actually felt slimmer and associated with that was an increase in confidence, irrespective of the fact that the other kids were still calling me the usual derogatory names I still felt much better, much braver and much happier and at least in my mind, much thinner. Seventy-two hours later on Saturday morning I eagerly stole another pill and unwaveringly swallowed it, even the repulsive pain that was imminent didn't serve as a deterrent. This time the backlash from the self-made monstrosity within me was even more despicable, this time it managed to escape through my throat in the form of caustic green bile which gushed uncontrollably from my mouth with a burning sensation that can only be described as vomiting sulphuric acid. The brutal physical reaction continued, another twelve hours of nil-by-mouth. The second barbaric assault on my own adolescent body was swiftly followed by a third on Sunday.

Almost twenty-four hours without any nutrition, of secretly discarding food I'd taken to my bedroom, of trying to play the part of a healthy active child, when internally my defences were at breaking point trying to defend the battery of the harsh and lethal appetite suppressants. Within ten days of that first fateful tablet I'd taken another five, giving me only four days grace without pain, although the remnants and consequences were prominent for the whole distasteful period. I was drained, pale, lacking in energy and drive, completely lifeless but I'd lost almost a stone in weight and it showed. I felt dead but my self-esteem was more alive than ever before. Then the damning reality, the bottle was empty, the Doctor annoyingly but not surprisingly told my Mother she was too early for her next prescription, to be precise six days too early, the six I stole had been noticed. Luckily blame was naturally levelled at the pharmacist, being the only link between the doctor and Mum, I mean where else could they have disappeared to it's not as if the kids were going to take them. Little did they know Michael was already on the road to prescribed addiction and the pharmacist was saddled with the missing tablets and was subsequently accused with short-changing my mum to make a profit from her loss. These pills were clearly expensive and any the pharmacist could skimp on would make him money. Upon receipt of the new bottle Mum emptied the contents and counted them out, there were thirty for thirty days consumption, it would appear the pharmacist had come to his senses and given the correct amount. My slimming plans, curiosity, abnormal appetite and freakish weight-loss had just come to a crashing halt. At the pinnacle of my renewed confidence and without any consideration for my mindset or shape my languid, secret delight was callously snatched away from me.

Another adventure in 'what if' curiosity had landed me with a huge conundrum to solve. Whilst other kids my age were plotting how to get out of doing homework, cheating in their exams, flirting with the opposite sex and dealing with prepubescent skin eruptions my main concern was how to get my hands on deadly weight-loss pills that had suddenly become inaccessible.

My world was gradually imploding as the need to inorganically lose weight with slimming pills was becoming a daily obsession.

It's utterly amazing how the mind can conjure images of despair when under stress, images and emotions that fundamentally serve to conceive resolutions.

I now know the pictures in our mind are a preview of life's forthcoming attractions, what you think about you can ultimately bring about, however back in the seventies with my obsessive problem and compulsion to lose weight those images were anything but pleasant.

The taste of blood on my lips was bitter, mixed with sweat and tears it had collected on its journey from my gaping head wound, the pain was searing, the trickle of blood endless. The last words I heard amongst the laughter and commotion from the hostile crowd, before the rock had made contact with my forehead were 'hey you, fat bastard', then Whack! The bludgeoning pain was excruciating as the blood gushed down my face. This and numerous other irrational images of potential violence, being painfully wounded and mental agony were plaguing me, they were becoming ingrained and recurring, I was destined to suffer and die as a bitter and aggrieved 'fat bastard'. The consequence of getting fatter and the ensuing physical and psychological persecution from my peers and society in general was driving me to total preposterous distraction and all because the appetite suppressants, those little tricolour man-made angels, my saviours from a cruel, hurtful world were now out of bounds and out of reach from my thieving podgy young hands. My mind was forcing me to come up with a solution and steal more pills. With such persuasive and graphic provocation it wasn't long before a bizarre but workable plot had unravelled itself.

Gingerly I pulled apart the two sections of the tricolour capsule, with a delicate twist out poured a white powder leaving two fragile but empty shells. The innovation lightbulb metaphorically positioned above my head was flashing with unstoppable erratic excitement, what a brilliant idea, what a beacon of inspiration. I would have smugly patted myself on the back but this was a very precise and graceful operation, one that was going to feed my obsession with enormous gratification, so I had to meticulously get it right, the repercussions of botching up this enterprising solution were unfathomable even by my overactive and creative mind. Into the empty shells and using a spatula from my junior chemistry set, I painstakingly poured another white powder, one that was slightly grainier than the one I had removed and then twisted the capsule shut. I proceeded to do the same with a further nine appetite suppressants, strenuously removing their contents and substituting them with another mysterious white substance. Once back in the bottle the ten counterfeit pills naturally looked like the remaining genuine ones, after all it was only the contents that had been swapped the tricolour shell was no different. This twisted master plan of deceit, danger and irreverence for my mother had my stomach doing adrenalin fuelled somersaults because not only had I conjured up a fool-proof plan but I had within my clutches ten potent magic beans, that ultimately were my salvation from a life of obesity and the degradation my unhealthy size was destined to bring.

In my bedroom in front of the window was a desk, the view sat from the desk was the length of a typical street in Coventry, the hustle and bustle of everyday ordinary life and ordinary people. From here I would stare down at the street and watch those inert goings-on with my customary curious and meddlesome thoughts. On my left was a wall-chart upon which the dates of ingesting the slimming pills, on alternate days through the month of July were plotted, this was over the course of twenty days denoted with a surreptitious 'SP' for 'slimming pill'. The perfect scheme to lose weight effortlessly even without the family pharmacist getting into trouble for skimping on Mum's medication.

Finally day twenty and as I sat at my desk smugly screeching a black marker cross through the last 'SP', I felt uneasy and nauseous, in fact the month of July had been a complete horrific nightmare. A ten tricolour capsule regime that probably shrunk my stomach to the size of a pea and had taken its toll on many areas of my life but even through the indescribable pain and sickness there was still a gloriously shining bright side to the bizarre ordeal I'd deliberately put myself through. My weight had plummeted along with the rolls of fat that had adorned my body no more than a few weeks ago. I was actually looking like a normal twelve year old boy and not like an overweight buffoon surrounded by little people. My acute vanity and the increase in self-confidence came at a dear price with severe consequences, an ulcerated stomach that plagues me to this day and a pain that has never been blanked out but that by any stretch of the imagination was just the tip of the iceberg, in reality my curiosity and experimentation with cannibalistic appetite suppressants heralded the first step of a unique, hazardous and destructive journey into the realms of searching and curiosity.

During that month of July whilst I was destroying my body, Mum was unknowingly taking the fake sugar pills, however extraordinarily continued to lose weight at the same pace as when she was whilst consuming the real pills and consequently reached her safe target weight. The Doctor ceased Mum's prescription largely because the dieting drugs were raising controversial questions in the media and months later went onto be completely banned in this country but also because she no longer needed them.

Precarious mass weight loss with ultra dangerous drugs stolen from my own Mother should have been the end of that potentially fatal journey, it had tragedy written all over it, it was

Motivation from a Tortured Mind

clearly a one way road to absolutely nowhere and yet it was the inception of an alternative new life, a macabre genesis, a deadly and obscure new beginning.

My fascination, eagerness and thirst for knowledge following the demented slimming interlude escalated at a frightening speed. The dark empires of my youthful imagination were in total overdrive, the 'what-if' syndrome was becoming an obsession, regularly challenging the realms of life, death, existence and purpose on this earth. These were probably not commonplace thoughts for a teenager but they plagued me night and day conjuring ideas from the offbeat to the distinctly grotesque, this was not going to be an ordinary summer.

The Weed-Killer

Beaming sunshine yellow ablaze with brightness almost with a golden glow, particularly against the exceptionally white porcelain of the toilet bowl, the regurgitating was relentless. Painfully scorching my throat with its acidity as it gushed from my stomach with an unbelievable mighty force, the taste was of molten steel almost like the taste of dentistry being spewed, thousands of molten teeth fillings pouring from my already damaged stomach. An unforgettable experience for my stomach, my throat and certainly my taste-buds not to mention the distinct yellowy staining left in the toilet. This was obsession out-of-control, the idiotic creation borne of acute curiosity, experimentation at its most lethal.

Chemistry Sets were very popular scientific toys with a range of colourful chemicals, test tubes, litmus papers, pipettes and the obligatory Bunsen burner, just enough to err on the side of safety but excite a young scientifically minded brain. This was one of the most exciting Christmas presents I'd ever had, however the experiments listed in the instruction manual were notably lame compared to what was going through my twisted mind. Once I'd completed the first experiment which demonstrated solubility using the chemical Copper

33

Sulphate, which basically involved dissolving it in water and trying to learn something from the fact it dissolved so readily and turned the water blue, my experimenting turned more sinister. After bolstering the feeble line-up of chemicals in the chemistry set with ones I'd misappropriated from chemistry lessons at school, my bedroom lab was capable of magical things like explosions which dented the ceiling and bizarrely entertaining oxidising chemical reactions full of colour, noise and poisonous gases. There are heinous criminals throughout history who started their evil regimes of death and destruction with less noxious and explosive materials, than I had displayed on my chemistry table in the comfort of my own bedroom. My intentions were never centred around harming people or in fact world domination, I was no megalomaniac just a maniac with a disproportionate sense of curiosity fired by the 'what-if' syndrome.

On this particular occasion merely weeks after the dreadful weight-loss episode, the question burning in my mind was 'what if I use one of those hollow left-over capsule shells fill it with a chemical from my home-made chemistry set and then judge the reaction in my body, if I swallow such a pill?'

Thirty minutes later I'm positioned head first in the toilet bowl and staring at the disgusting but bright result of doing such a ridiculous thing, with endless throat stinging and stomach churning yellow vomit. I can still taste the gross experience today of ingesting a fatal chemical just to judge the physical reaction, a chemical which shockingly years later became a vital ingredient in household weed killers.

What did this latest escapade teach me? Other than if you orally take poisonous chemicals you vomit ferociously, the colour can be quite fetching based on which chemical you consume and animal testing wasn't necessary because a human test concluded weed-killer was not for eating.

It certainly wasn't an education more of a stepping-stone to further inquisitiveness on the precarious road of 'what-if', naturally leading to further curiosity bound circumstances and associated issues. Nevertheless, every experience, every situation no matter how obscure, inconceivable and bizarre constitutes another autobiographical building block of our mentality, personality and complexion of our character.

Demons & Lepers

Throughout most of her life Mother was riddled with health challenges most of which were a direct result of obesity and I'm assuming the lack of exercise, just because in all my youth I never saw her partake in any physical activity. In most cases Doctors of the age simply prescribed magical solutions with badly scrawled prescriptions, almost every ailment known to man was dealt with drugs and excruciatingly bad hand-writing. I remember Doctors scribbling the prescriptions before they even looked up to see who was addressing them and long before their patients had even finished describing their symptoms. That slap-dash generic approach to medicine explains why Mum had been prescribed lethal appetite suppressants, as an alternative to the real support she desperately needed in tackling her acute obesity with exercise and healthier eating. The same applied to treating her severe insomnia, instead of establishing the root of the problem she was eagerly prescribed noxious barbiturates and without further consultation they were administered via repeat prescription. The ease with which such lethal drugs could be procured was ludicrous, considering that particular form of barbiturate is currently banned in the UK and has been for over two decades that alone demonstrates the farce of its usage and availability back then. For drug addicts and serial users of such substances the laughable system was an absolute pushover, however that wasn't the only drawback of a facile and lenient medicine world. There were unrecorded casualties, other than medical dependency and abuse from junkies, such as scheming curious teenagers who couldn't resist the temptation of another set of tri-coloured capsules, which were just begging to be tested on an already blemished and injured young body.

My curiosity and temptation was unbearable. I needed to know how such a small capsule containing an insipid white powder could induce relentless sleep within thirty minutes of taking it. Mum used to joke about its effect, that she would sleep through an earthquake once the capsule had been taken and in her quirky humorous way referring to them as 'nightly slices of death'. The sleeping pills were alive they were goading me, calling out my name, pondering whether I was indeed brave enough to witness a night of death.

The inevitable happened, a single barbiturate meant for adult consumption to remedy chronic insomnia found its way into my body, a body that had already been aggrieved with harsh appetite suppressants and deadly weed-killer and my only hesitancy was I didn't want to sleep through an earthquake because I would miss the ensuing drama of its destruction.

There was no procrastination from the grim reaper as he wasted no time in swiftly galloping to my bedroom and eradicating fourteen full hours of adolescent life. Yet another revelation in my nurturing years, a capsule that could temporarily wipe out life for a whole night and nonchalantly leave you in an after-life zombie limbo, for a further twelve hours. I was floating with little relevance to night or day and entered a second night of blissful sleep, from which I awoke reborn with an acute freshness I'd never witnessed.

Unlike the appetite suppressants these magic little wonders didn't appear to have hugely negative side effects, no pain no vomiting just a bite of death for one night, followed by a hollow brain feeling the day after, followed by heavenly sleep on the second night, followed by an almighty explosion of energy and life.

Rather favourably they were also easily counterfeited and that's exactly what happened next, over time I replaced fifteen capsules with everyday sugar. Three weeks of experimentation later I was getting rather bored with the soporific effect the barbiturates were having, nevertheless I was already contemplating the next raucous adventure. If one single capsule had such an effect that practically lasted over twenty four hours, what would be the effect of taking two at the same time? Very soon I discovered the answer. The slice of death still only lasted approximately fourteen hours however the zombie spin-off sequence upon waking was more severe than before, I was almost drifting between life and death, practically half-dead for a full twelve hours. It bordered on hallucinogenic, dreaming whilst awake, everything was in soft focus with light blurring the edges, voices were in slow motion my own body registered a slower pace, albeit my physical movements were regular. I was walking on the moon, in an airless atmosphere. It was clearly a small step for mankind but a gargantuan colourful but decelerated step for me. There was only one way to go on this road to exploration, the magic number was THREE. My adrenalin feverishly pumped all day, it was Friday and most kids felt the same, the difference was they were getting ready for a weekend of childish shenanigans and I was preparing to swallow three poisonous sleeping pills, probably possessing enough power to kill a horse. I was so excited I'd even lost my appetite, huh who needed appetite suppressants, those days were long gone. I'd planned a faultless strategy, take them early to get through the boring deathly sleeping part, wake on Saturday morning to a weekend of drug infused floating half-existence, which by my calculations would diminish during Sunday night and I would wake bright and breezy on Monday morning for the week ahead at school, a perfect plan for a perfect dreamy weekend.

Finally 9pm arrived, the scheduled time to swallow three barbiturates. Through the swirl of excitement and anticipation in my already drug riddled brain, there was no recollection of getting changed or even climbing into bed but when I finally woke at Midday on Saturday, fifteen hours of deep sleep later, I still felt like I could sleep for the rest of my life. Reluctantly I gazed into the bathroom mirror not knowing what manner of deathly expression would be adorning my face, I wasn't disappointed. I looked like I felt, all my internal organs had been through a miraculous transfusion. Somewhere in the world a hundred year old man had woke with a new lease of life and was crazily jumping around in ecstatic energy contradicting his ageing dead skin, while his festering diseased organs were implanted within this teenager. On the outside I was fourteen on the inside entering my one hundred and first year. That included my mind which was thirty seconds behind my body and could barely recall the ability to put one foot after the other in order to walk. Even through the melodramatic mental numbing I was experiencing a minute particle of my mischievous brain was ticking over and writing the next fatal chapter. I could hear and feel the plan constructing and rapidly unfolding as the long, dark corridors in my head became more sinister, more unpredictable and dangerously more palpable.

Within all of us there are sleeping demons that will breathe their fire and destruction when insecurities awaken and revitalise them, along with dormant lepers that spend our entire lifetimes waiting to trawl their carnage through our thoughts, invigorated, fuelled and energised only with negative emotions. We avoid these monsters at all costs and only ever reluctantly stumble across them as we go through the trials and tribulations of our lives. The only deterrent is a positive attitude fired by an insatiable desire, which is the equivalent to obliterating a cake with a rapidly firing machine gun, it really wouldn't be recognisable after an explosive flurry of dedicated bullets, that's the power of desire. On the contrary, Bang! Bang! Bang! I was ferociously beating down the doors to their incarcerated existence, my brain was awash with their cancerous, baneful compulsion to lash into life and leave no stone of decent being unturned.

A resilient and powerfully corrosive army of demons and lepers were marching forward victorious in their war of temptation versus repulsion, curiosity versus indifference and ultimately good versus evil, it was a foregone conclusion a futile fight as desire was the unanimous force on their side. Desire was creating an underlying catalytic power for temptation, curiosity and evil. There was no escape from this one way tunnel to darkness, the army with their might, momentum and ravenous appetite were supporting and pushing me to the next big black hole of unknown consequences.

I bravely fought my heavy leaden eyelids shutting on a bright world full of rightful promise, immense potential and youthful exuberance, as my physical ability to grasp everyday reality and teenage normality diminished at break-neck speed. The demons and lepers that cheered so loudly were dormant again their war was over as this simple, predisposed battle had been won with the razor sharp sword of desire. Calm was restored the very second the jeering monsters achieved their effortless goal, the ominous, fateful doom of swallowing TEN barbiturates. Ten individual portions of death, only four less than the years I'd been fortunate enough to have life in my veins, the very veins that now had poison gushing through them, a harsh sleep inducing poison that was engrossed in stopping the beat of my heart, extensive brain damage, followed by an instantaneous loss of life.

Suicide wasn't the purpose of the mass overdose. I categorically didn't want to meet the grim reaper. It was merely a macabre experiment into the unknown. Nevertheless, I wasn't expecting a mammoth debilitating coronary followed by a two week coma, had I known that would be the gruesome outcome I may have invented other methods of satisfying my incessant curiosity. The 'mystery illness' that shaped much of my thinking, attitude and behaviour through its near-death experience was self-inflicted. I woke to a joyous family, staring through square panes of glass in a magnolia wall, a family that had witnessed two weeks of convulsions. They were only slightly less baffled than the doctors who had given a less than fifty percent chance of survival and even less chance of survival without brain-damage. Miraculously and to the utter astonishment of the medical world I survived with absolutely no long lasting repercussions, however my bizarre, unconventional journey into the many facets of life had only just begun. Already by the tender age of fourteen my curiosity had fuelled many unsavoury actions from stealing my Mother's medicine, to inexplicably cheating death itself after inducing it with a homicidal overdose.

The Exorcist

A skeletal frame, long tousled greasy beard and a bald head covered with a flimsy white cotton turban, deep set haunting eyes that stared straight into your soul, tearing it into shreds without any effort. Swathed in white cotton cloths he sat relentlessly for hours on end in the precarious lotus position, on my bed. That summer, hoards of people came to my bedroom where the ceiling tiles still bore the stains and damage from exploding experiments carried out with my chemistry set, to visit this puny, inconsequential, scruffy man. Not only did they visit him in abundance they paid thousands for the privilege, for he offered them salvation from evil.

Most God-fearing Asian cultures believe there is a dark, deathly calamitous side to the world, one inhabited by unearthly abominations, demons devils and hellish satanic creatures that fiendishly stalk the Earth and contemplate its destruction, whilst causing untold and continuing misery to mankind. These inanimate monstrosities are effortlessly conjured into the real world for the pursuance of inflicting pain, torment and suffering onto individuals, by people versed in the art of sorcery and Satanism. An alarmingly disproportionate amount of people believe such black magic is rife and completely responsible for a whole host of atrocious medical conditions, ghastly apparitions and abnormal behavioural patterns. Rather than seek medical, psychological or psychiatric attention they involve exorcists and such characters that are conversant with expelling curses and ridding people of misfortune and afflictions caused by infernal poltergeists and satanic demons, that have been sacrilegiously summoned by humans for the one and only purpose of causing harm to others.

The insignificant, bony individual adorning my sleeping space was one such exorcist, allegedly competent in tackling the evilness of the dark side and the inflictions that depraved devil practise caused. But why was he sat on my bed?

Four months had passed since my ill-fated experimentation with sleeping pills and for four long months my parents searched high and low for an explanation. They had abandoned the medical world after much consultation, the most doctors and child illness specialists managed was the usual dumfounded expressions and names of other medical practitioners that we should consult with. My deliberate overdose became an infamous conundrum, blood test after blood test and still they found nothing, not even a hint of what caused my impromptu relapse, luckily for me not even traces of the lethal drug I'd taken. Mum and Dad were at the end of their tether and as a penultimate resort before calling upon the bony exorcist, were forced down the inglorious route of meeting a soothsayer. For a formidable contribution of cash this medium who was in cahoots with the dark world of sorcery, scared the living daylights out of us. It took him five minutes to ascertain I was the epitome of evil and that he could see a destructive demon inside me, the very one that had caused my mysterious collapse. The beast was gradually destroying my life its mission was simple, my untimely death and despair for my family. The medium swiftly grabbed the cash and promptly ordered us out of his spooky, musty house, apparently the devil inside me was causing him a deep upsetting pain and to make matters worse there was now a spine-chilling black crow sat on my shoulder that was staring at him determined to destroy his soul. We didn't need to be told twice, particularly as he grabbed his sword and started to swing it in our direction in order to protect himself from the malicious crow. Whatever happened that day, from his shocking change of voice, rolling eyes, to his frothing mouth convinced my parents that demonic skulduggery was to blame for my demise, so they unhesitatingly made contact with the wretched being now residing in my bedroom. They were desperate and it's amazing to what lengths desperate people will go to. Who could have predicted my curious nature and unwavering desire to meddle with my body using my own Mother's pilfered illicit drugs, would summon one of India's leading experts in the battle against witchcraft and demons, along with a plethora of his disciples, who all had cursed lives of their own that desperately needed his virtuoso attention.

A run-of-the-mill Sunday afternoon in summery England with everyday ordinary people relaxing their bloated bodies after over indulging on their Sunday roast dinners. Our house was clearly not run-of-the-mill, with a queue of people patiently waiting for a consultation with the swarthy exorcist, fourteen crates of milk in the kitchen, that's approximately three hundred individual bottles of milk and all around the house wherever there was a sink, outlet or drain, which included the back-garden and the external toilet, there were people of all ages, shapes and sizes from the decrepit old and infirm to tiny toddlers who could barely walk, violently vomiting, in fact actually straining their stomachs and happily regurgitating the disgusting contents.

Throughout history individuals with unique skills and expertise in the least understood subjects have often been often revered, celebrated and admired, when such exclusive understanding is married to something people fear, undoubtedly such experts can withhold a certain sense of power over people. Such a commanding influence can lead to outlandish beliefs and devotees that will undertake almost anything the prodigies suggest or recommend.

Our mysterious guest clearly had a substantial reputation in the fight against the much feared subject of black magic and other such ungodly practices. Clearly the belief in this unholy area was rife hence people were flocking to my bedroom to visit this unlikely saviour.

Inflicted being after inflicted being drifted in for his knowledgeable advice from mentally crippled people to individuals simply down on their luck and each one of them were overcome with joy at his unearthly omnipotent presence, he commanded their respect and naturally thousands of pounds in fees for his consultations. As each one with a huge sigh of relief bowed at his lotus positioned body, he achingly stretched out his skeletal arms and touched their temples, without being asked they closed their eyes and let his penetrating stare bore into their minds. On each occasion he identified a poltergeist or evil demon and conversed with the malicious entities, while the rest of the crammed crowd in my bedroom listened with terror-stricken expressions. He spat out venom and obscenities condemning the unwelcome forces and denounced their existence banishing them back to hell. While my friends were mischievously playing in the park, annoying their neighbours with childish pranks and cautiously chatting to girls, I was waiting for my personal exorcism, for my very own devil to be sentenced back to the underworld. To make matters even worse every single blighted soul that visited our house had heard about my personal infliction and looked upon me with painful pity, in a way that suggested my condition was terminal and that my days on earth were numbered.

The conclusion for each one of the exorcist's damned patients was identical, whilst his conversation with their resident spooks had allegedly stunned them into stillness, they had to be physically removed from the body, this was done through the process of spewing their guts up, however not simply by forcefully sticking their fingers down their throats but by drinking a whole cauldron of specially prepared warm milk. Each cauldron contained six pints of milk, which was gently heated and then carried to his side, where a privileged assistant from the crowd stirred the milk with a very large silver spoon, whilst the exorcist predictably swore at the demons and belittled their presence within his patient. Once the ten minutes of verbal abuse ceased and the entities were reportedly stunned, the equally stunned patient carried the milk to the nearest toilet or drain and began the process of drinking it, upon drinking the milk there was vomiting, in which the occupying evil was expelled. Naturally, the mere thought of drinking six pints of warm milk, whilst being terrified there is a demon lurking within you is enough to make anyone vomit uncontrollably, however in many cases the disgusting regurgitations happened at the very moment the first gulps were taken, even then the poor sods had to drink the whole lot, otherwise according to the exorcist the live-in ghouls would not be extracted in their entirety. People believed in the exorcist and carried out his absurd instructions without any hesitation whatsoever.

After three days of these bizarre activities with a multitude of possessed people and non-stop talk of Satan, black magic and evil goings-on, coupled with the berserk honour people felt of meeting this famed saviour, the already thin line between reality and fantasy was becoming increasingly blurred. I was beginning to believe I had my own personal demon, that maybe all the unlikely shenanigans I'd created weren't my fault at all, that maybe my hand was literally forced by an evil being that was controlling and gradually destroying my life, even to the point where my fatal, experimental overdose that resulted in this dubious exorcist being sat on my bed healing people, was a direct result of the devil himself.

The fourth and final day of his hypnotic visit arrived and it was now my turn to be sat in front of him, I was his final patient and I was shockingly ready and thoroughly convinced it was time to rid my young, self-battered body of the evil residing within it. The almost comical unholy ritual began, with my inconceivable but full mental and physical permission, as he eerily announced to the thirty transfixed people sat in my bedroom that this last purification would take all he's got, this was pure unimaginable evil with an unsurpassed power and a forceful possession over my soul, like he had never witnessed before. At that moment in time I actually believed him.

The cauldron of warm milk arrived and a random guest volunteered to stir it while the exorcist prepared himself for his final and toughest battle against evil, before returning home to his native India. His eyes were closed but I felt he was still staring, I could feel the burn of his gaze almost as if his shut eyelids were an illusion and in reality they were starkly piercing into my brain. I preferred them shut because when he finally opened them they were painfully blood red, with the kind of petrified expression I could only associate with someone who had just received the death penalty, someone about to have their final breath forcefully taken from them and prematurely about to enter the frightening unknown world of death.

That dreaded moment of judgement, that unless your death is instant and without hesitation, we could all potentially witness, when poignant slices of your entire life flash heartbreakingly past your eyes, your torturous autobiography reaching its final chapter before your life is whipped away into the darkness. That was the dramatic calamity flickering past my eyes, all my momentous moments of infamy and shame captured in one agonizing, emotional reel of mental film as the exorcist pressed my temples and burnt his gaze into me, it was almost as if he was watching the drama of my inappropriate career in wrong doing unfold. My evil memoirs came to a crashing halt at the precise moment when I swallowed the unearthly quantity of sleeping pills, the vision was lucid capturing every iota of emotion and movement as if it was all happening again, I was struggling to move on from those shameful images of deception, I couldn't he wouldn't let me. The exorcist had fast-forwarded my abominable life and was now scrutinising the humiliating footage, like a forensic scientist studying criminal fingerprints, he was well and truly onto me with a humongous magnifying glass. This cheating flagrant teenage rat was about to be ceremoniously captured. My contemptible secrets and disgraceful behaviour that had been the cause of so much anguish, pain and heartbreak were being degradingly revealed. The exorcist spouted out a venomous string of distasteful obscenities that in normal circumstances would raise more than an eyebrow of distaste. He had located and isolated the evil demon within me. I was clearly off the hook as the very entity responsible for my reprehensible actions had been finally found lurking in my soul and blamed for all my felonies. I could sense the shock and panic of the crowd witnessing this surreal drama unwind, they were petrified beyond belief. The blasphemous dialogue between the exorcist and the demon continued. I could hear the monster's silent voice reverberating deep within my bones as it bitterly argued with the exorcist and blatantly refused to leave my body. With a final scathing condemnation the demon was sentenced back to hell, the exorcist released my head and collapsed in exhaustion, the fight was over, good had conquered evil and it was time for me to drink six pints of sick-inducing warm milk.

I felt cleansed, as if a tumultuous burden had been lifted or was it simply relief that I hadn't been unmasked for the enormous shameless and wicked scoundrel that I was. Either way, I was sat in front of a cauldron of warm milk with concerned family, friends and incidental strangers waiting patiently for me to drink it and expel the now temporarily dormant but nevertheless fiendish possession, concealed within my body.

I didn't have the time or the mental capacity to consider this crazy situation, after all the theatrics I was drained, even of my cynical attitude. It just seemed natural to take a huge gulp of milk, not that I had any choice in the matter, especially considering the eager goading crowd of believers surrounding me.

Minutes before a volcano erupts there is a ground rumbling vibration as the lava underneath the surface gathers pressure, this serves as a warning whilst the volcano is preparing to gush uncontrollably into the air. Within ten seconds of the warm milk landing in my stomach, I witnessed the same warning rumble, something wasn't quite right, a gulp of milk shouldn't have such a disproportionate reaction, the pain was agonising as my midriff was clearly trembling, my body was cramping, I couldn't hold back the painful tears any longer, people were holding onto me trying to stabilise me from rocking my body to help alleviate the dreadful sickness I was feeling but they were still encouraging me to drink even more milk. The demon was putting up a substantial fight, it didn't want to leave, it had no choice this was exorcised milk, specially stirred to eradicate evil unwanted entities. Suddenly and without warning the steaming demonic load from my stomach gushed with a searing heat through my pipes and with considerate projectile force shot from my mouth and hit the floor, missing the drain and subsequently splashing the distressed onlookers. Mouthful after mouthful of foul brownie red vileness came gushing out, completely unequal to the food I'd consumed, there seemed to be no end to the acidic oral excrement being expelled from my body, I was almost expecting a round of applause as it finally stopped and they patted my back for reassurance, that my personal incumbent devil had permanently been dismissed back to the hellish abyss where it came from.

There was one further consultation with the exorcist, in which he confirmed I was now devoid of demons, my accursed nightmare was conclusively over. My parents paid his extortionate fees and he left the country.

Stories of sorcery, evil goings-on and vomiting huge quantities of milk were rife in the community, it seemed the burden of black magic and it's appalling mental and physical consequences had been lightened for many ill-fated people, whilst the Exorcist had legitimately created immense wealth for himself on this trip alone, it was clearly a worthy cause considering how many individuals were now bizarrely relieved and cured of whatever ailments were hurting them and stifling their damned lives. In my obtuse and intermittently curious mind there was an ongoing feud between reality and fantasy, this whole unimaginable and agonisingly strange experience had left my brain wracked with question after question, particularly based around how the entirety of the situation was self-inflicted, wholly created and caused by my inquisitiveness. To be precise it was the unexpected chain reaction from a huge and deliberate overdose.

Was this hateful debacle the work of a selfish, egocentric narcissistic child completely aware of his calculated actions, or had his heinous self-destructive and loathsome behaviour been influenced and forced by an evil force within? Such a force unknown to man, science or common-sense, a force summoned from the darkest, deepest depths of the unknown, a force which stood for everything sinful, damnable and clearly the complete antithesis of God and all that is perceived as good and wholesome?

Three months had now passed since the communal vomiting sessions, as each day subsided further questions of reality versus fantasy arose, there was just no escaping the mental debate and angst this was causing. Reality was fuelled by science, in which unknown territories of damnation or even God simply don't exist, everything has a scientific explanation, every word of God and Satan can be succinctly explained and opposed with education, knowledge and the lifelong study of scientists. However, tales of everyday people now living totally cured and satisfied lives because they chose to drink six pints of milk in Coventry and then projectile vomit their stomachs to an audience of excited, convinced onlookers were of epidemic proportions, including one particular story chronicling the unfortunate condition of infertility. The Exorcist had even managed to cure the unfortunate inability to have children, the married couple in question had been unsuccessful for four whole years, one program of treatment from the bearded oddity and three months later the woman was clearly pregnant and the expectant family overjoyed and in unquestionable awe of his heavenly, god-sent ability.

In my vastly developing teenage mind I was beginning to accept the reality of an unknown world, that had eluded science and general common-sense thinking, a virtual world governed by inhuman, inanimate forces that were either yet to be discovered by the scientific, mathematical and methodical world or had been deliberately ignored and whitewashed as there wasn't an acceptable explanation for such evil, in the same diabolical ignorance that science denies the existence of God.

Our general thoughts and the words we use in everyday conversation have an instantaneous level of planning, in other words in most conversations electrical impulses rush at lightning speed through the brain split seconds before words are spouted from our mouths. The words we use are either reactive or proactive, we're either responding to someone else's words or we're creating words based on our thoughts, experiences or stimuli. That's the art and ability of conversation, one fortunately we're all blessed with. There are infrequent times when our capacity and mastery of saying the things we want to and avoid saying the wrong things are severely tested. Those infrequent times usually occur with the involvement of emotions, namely emotions such as excitement, frustration, petulance, sorrow and anger. If you've ever said something you wish you hadn't and we've all been in that retrospective situation, it's usually been exacerbated by an extreme emotion, particularly when we're involved in an argument. Imagine how many secrets, truths and insults have been uncontrollably spouted in moments of anger and resentment, immediately resulting in regrets, revelations and awkwardness and in certain cases irreparable consequences and untold damage. Sometimes a choice of controversial words can alter the direction and perception of hundreds of people, our history is riddled with such erroneous or premeditated dialogues. The pen is undoubtedly mightier than the sword and used in disgruntlement and anger can cause utmost pain, suffering and angst, literally decapitating the individual listener or recipients of the monologue.

An argument that callously decapitated an entire belief and faith system ended with the simple anger generated statement of 'you fucking fool, he slept with me!' In isolation this blasé announcement was insignificant and completely harmless and yet in context resulted in obliterating what thousands of innocent victims believed and the necessarily lengthy incarceration of a particular hirsute, vomit inducing exorcist.

It so transpired the cure for infertility, which I recall was administered over a two week period with curtains drawn and in total privacy considering the encroaching demon destroying the barren woman was one of the most powerful and it was a hazard to her well-being having others, including her husband present, was to personally and regularly impregnate her. Her obvious drowsiness following each private session wasn't the tiredness caused by an over-active, fierce resident entity fighting hard against expulsion from her infertile body, more like an over-active penis belonging to a charlatan who had access to relaxants that he duly plied her with. Somewhere in the world today is the illegitimate, thirty-something offspring of a crook, an apathetic shyster who was in fact the real demon preying upon the vulnerabilities of Devil fearing people searching for unorthodox remedies against everyday mental and physical afflictions. As for the comical and extraordinary vomit inducing ritual, one that was instrumental in convincing me there was the possibility of satanic interference in my life, there was anything but exorcism and medicinal magic at play. In reality the swindling phony was unsuspectingly dropping a small quantity of an arsenic based drug into the warm milk, which was then innocently stirred in by the volunteering stirrer, a quantity small enough to cause extreme regurgitation but barely enough to cause ongoing sickness or death.

The ingenious rouse made the so-called exorcist into a millionaire, albeit he was shamefully exposed, duly investigated, trialled and subsequently jailed, he made people believe he was offering a cure and that power of faith and belief he instigated into people not only actually cured them, it instilled into my mind the gargantuan potential of personal BELIEF and how above many attributes one can possess, it single-handedly forms the beginning and ongoing sustainability of achievement.

The crook was emphatically plying innocent people with a deadly poison that was potentially more harmful than any possible good it could do, it caused irrepressible frantic vomiting, a poison so noxious it was traditionally used to murder people or even commit suicide. Those involuntary regurgitations concreted the credibility of the crook therefore creating positive, formidable and secure belief and thought patterns within the minds of his victims, they comprehensively accepted they were being cured and yet in reality they were simply being contaminated with a toxin and being relieved of vast amounts of money which they willingly gave. The stronghold his credulous exorcisms had over people initiated well-being, relief and remedy in everything from migraines and simple aches and pains to rehabilitation of posture and walking deficiencies and cataclysmic mental inadequacies.

*'There are times when one just has to
press the allegorical button, irrespective of what
the outcome may be, of course there are times
when it'll be regretful but there will also be times
when it's the best possible thing you could have
done. Taking those somewhat precarious chances
elude from locating your own personal buttons,
that when metaphorically pressed, present the
life you truly want, entwined with the emotions
that catalyse it into action.'*

CHAPTER 2

Belief

'It's the shining, lighthouse beacon that relentlessly lights the path to your personal utopia, your promised land your infinite wishes and fantasies. It's your incessant blinding light at the end of the tunnel.'

Through the realms of history there are multitudes of faiths, leaders and charismatic swindlers that have altered the perceptions and beliefs of millions of people, whether they are entire religions, systems of belonging and acceptance, demonic cults or simply influential people that have the ability to indoctrinate others into a certain way of behaving or thinking. Such people, systems and dogmas have not only resulted in the extremities of war, blood-shed resulting in the vast destruction of life and civilization and appalling atrocities against other human-beings but been instrumental in creating masses of positivity, huge personal achievement, immense creativity, immeasurable success and above all HOPE.

Personal belief in your own ability to achieve whatever you desire inoculates you against the pitfalls and stumbling blocks on the sometimes long and precarious road to your chosen destination. If you truly believe in yourself, that you are genuinely worthy enough, great enough, substantially spirited in your dexterity and aptitude, blessed with the foresight and laser-like vision of where you want to be and what you want to have with blindingly crystal clear clarity, then you will possess the necessary hope, strength and endurance to get there.

Your personal belief will by the mere nature of its intricate and vulnerable thought based mental construction come under regular and sometimes forceful attack at every possible juncture. Why? Because your belief is the compound effect of your ongoing thinking and your habitual thoughts and irrespective of the strength of what you believe in, there will always be an opposing negative that will periodically ambush your assurance and chip away at your confidence and faith. It's almost human nature for us to contemplate the very worst of life, to continually speculate and surmise a situation of counteractive incongruity. Unless, you've nonchalantly strolled through life without a single hint of antagonism, adversity or cynicism ensconced in your brain and without people who represent any or all three, your mind has every imaginable contradiction, contrary hostility, human-kind disaster and impropriety accumulated and poised to take aim and fire at your beliefs on a daily basis.

If that's the case then it's not your belief, assuming you have one that becomes the issue, in fact it's the successful and perpetual defence and barricading of your beliefs that is paramount.

Your belief is the solid brick built castle, a stronghold of expectation, faith, opinion, confidence, credence and hope, a concrete and secure construction epitomising the very things you stand for, breathe for and live for. Each solid brick represents ambition, anticipation, aspiration and optimism. It's the shining, lighthouse beacon that relentlessly lights the path to your personal utopia, your promised land your infinite wishes and fantasies. It's your incessant blinding light at the end of the tunnel. Every waking minute, of every hour, of every day your personal citadel of belief is under the threat of aggression and attack, almost everything from your emotional history, your environment, your everyday thinking is an enemy and each encounter, strike and raid on your castle loses one of your bricks and leaves a vulnerable gaping hole in your belief stronghold, a hole that weakens your stance and resistance to the arrows of negativity that are mercilessly fired directly and ferociously through every chasm created in your castle. Belief is repeatedly accessible and susceptible to attack with our own constitution, environment, company and character shooting the arrows. Each anti-belief arrow makes the void even greater.

'The streets in this country are no longer safe, every time you step out you do so at your own peril, our society is spiralling out of control, where people, in many cases very young disconnected people are plotting your demise and won't think twice about you or the consequences of their crime against you, before they violently attack you for the spare change in your pockets, I can categorically tell you I've never felt so unsafe or disheartened in my own country ever before.'

That was an actual statement made by an esteemed political figure in the United Kingdom in 2007. How would that make you feel as the reader of such a statement, particularly if you're a resident of the said country? There is a huge possibility it's a completely true picture of the state of the nation, in which case undoubtedly it could save you from an abhorrent, ugly scenario, if nothing else it'll give you a sense of heightened awareness which can only be good for your personal safety. On the other hand it represents a typical environmental encroachment of your belief, immediately upon reading the statement you feel threatened, under attack and in some cases frightened to step out of your own front-door.

Every single day there is a discriminatory and often brutal intrusion of your belief, it's a daily battle of arrows, bullets, torpedoes, grenades and in the case of the political statement above a cannon-ball shot at your bastion of belief. That single cannon-ball fired by a politician who was probably innocently sharing his personal experiences and judgement, blasted a handful of bricks into oblivion and left a cavernous hole in your stronghold. I actually recall reading the statement and it mentally disturbed me into contemplating the reality of being mugged and stabbed by teenagers who wanted my belongings. Those painful and disturbing images caused me untold calamity because I could actually picture the scene of lying in the street with bleeding wounds. One simple, careless, righteous declaration from a faceless, insignificant politician traumatised my mind into imagining the potential loathsome consequences of stepping out of my own home. I witnessed the suffering of a malicious encounter which in reality was very unlikely to happen. Now that may well have through the sense of heightened awareness, saved me from such a malodorous situation, the flipside was I suffered the mental agony of it anyway.

The reality of a genuine attack is largely incomprehensible however reading one single sentence in a newspaper which was probably forgotten a few days later, actually left an indelible imprint within my subconscious mind, an indelible imprint that affected my belief and could potentially affect my future judgement, actions and outcomes, in other words my castle may have lost a brick FOREVER.

A lost, damaged or vulnerable brick in your personal bastion, stronghold of belief can only weaken your defences to the ongoing daily lambasting your belief receives and undoubtedly can alter your thinking, your agility and your entire direction.

The antithesis of the daily lifelong attacks against our stronghold is it fortifies our defences and arms and strengthens our resolve. It's a natural rejuvenation and bolstering of our immunity. In the same way the medical world injects patients with a form of the very virus they're being protected from, the attacks against our belief inoculate us against future onslaughts of the same kind.

Every individual on this planet withstanding any unfortunate conditions or illness is born equal and is indistinguishable in their embryonic potential to any other individual that takes their first breath of life. However that rudimentary breath of irrefutable equilibrium is where that impartiality to the future dramatically alters. The environment, circumstances, parentage and legacy one is born into starts to make an impression on our beliefs and future as soon as that initial crying breath of air is taken. As we cannot predetermine where we are born and who our parents are, we cannot control or perceive the influences that will determine our early formative years. Without exception every single microscopic happening in our lives has a direct or inadvertent effect on our entire lifetime.

In the same way we're born with organs, genes and limbs our mindset is born with an identical stack of belief bricks as every other human, from the moment we come into this world we lose and gain bricks with each and every occurrence our lives witness or encounters.

Belief is the unmitigated, simplest form of mental representation. It's a psychological state in which an individual holds a proposition or premise to be true, one of the integral building bricks of conscious thought itself, therefore capable of radically affecting your mindset, attitude, confidence and ultimately your success.

Any achievement of any magnitude requires the achiever to believe it can be accomplished, that they are indeed capable of bringing their goal to a successful conclusion. A half-hearted attempt will always produce half-hearted, lacklustre results, therefore strengthening your stronghold irrespective of how many bricks you lose, through the consistent and daily violation of your belief is absolutely paramount.

Each brick in your belief bastion is a war-torn hero in its own right, it's suffered anything from a skirmish to a bloody battle to be where it proudly sits, forming the foundations and construction of your stronghold, its material strength, architecture, durability and stamina is directly commensurate to the battle, bloodshed, angst and emotions it's been through. You will have susceptible bricks that habitually fracture and fall when under attack from life's inevitable anti-belief grenades, these might just be fledgling, feeble beliefs that still need to mature and become sturdier or in the worse case scenario the bludgeoning you get may be so astringent, forbidding and vile it makes the most guarded, powerful and stalwart of bricks crumble at first impact.

From that first infant breath belief is built and destroyed, cleansed and corrupted, beautified and deformed, smoothed and contorted, straightened and warped. Every hour, every day something or someone will light it or darken it, gradually creating the entities we become, the things we do, the way we act and the successes and failures we experience.

There are times the very people wrecking our belief systems are the ones that care the most. *'Dad, when I grow up I want to be an astronaut and fly in a rocket', 'Well Son, that takes years of work and only one in a million ever gets there'* That wasn't a particularly negative, caustic or derogatory reply, however in an instant the child has just had a belief-brick bludgeoned by a caring parent who actually told the truth, in fact he was absolutely right, it does take years to be an astronaut and only one in a million actually fulfils such a role, nevertheless it's unlikely that particular child will be the one in a million that makes it. Most parents through their supportive, ingrained and systematic natures may make such nonchalant and seemingly harmless statements to help children avoid disappointment and are innocently said without a second thought and certainly without any malice. Worse such apathetic utterances are aired because the parents may themselves truly belief such an achievement is impossible, hence they've passed on their own intimidated beliefs onto their children.

There could be a multitude of reasons why that child never becomes an astronaut, all things considered it's one of the many childlike, naive fantasies children have. Nevertheless, despite the enormous complications, education, discipline and effort required to accomplish the intrepid role of an astronaut the child in this synopsis is one belief-brick less likely. A miniscule alteration to the same statement could have made a universe of difference *'Well Son that takes years of work and only one in a million ever gets there but if you really want to be an astronaut you can be'*. Whether that child ever becomes an astronaut or not those extra twelve effortless words at the end of the sentence have just bolstered a belief-brick. The actual effect of the statement and the bolstering is almost immeasurable, however enough of those positive affirmations will not only inoculate that child from the inevitable life-long knocks coming his way, it can also be instrumental in many other unequivocal, positive attainments. *'You can be'* represents everything from immunisation against belief attacks to a glimmering ray of hope and irrespective of how diminutive the addition to the statement was, the overall effect ranges from a tiny iota of beneficial difference to a constructive and monumental change in perspective, attitude and strength.

This certainly isn't a lesson in positive parenting, it's an example of how even innocuous care-free comments flippantly bandied around by our own Mother's and Father's will have innocently bombarded our belief and affected our lives. It perfectly demonstrates the daily life-long struggles our belief has had to endure, from the very moment we appeared unblemished into existence sporting a huge stack of belief-bricks, an identical quantity to anyone else entering this world, to wherever we are and whatever situation we currently find ourselves in today.

Understanding this logic of belief draws three decisive assertions:

1. Your Belief is paramount in achieving everything from your ambitions to building and supporting your morale, confidence and self-esteem. Therefore forms the central nucleus, foundation and cornerstone of your philosophy, perception and perseverance.

2. Your Belief has been affected positively or negatively throughout your entire life and is the compound repercussion of every damaging, repairing, bolstering,

battering or supporting comment, situation or occurrence that has ever happened to you.

3. The bruised, contaminated, destroyed and deteriorated bricks in your belief castle have to be unequivocally fixed, replaced or compensated for, before you travel speedily and without hesitation in the direction of your dreams, aspirations and psychological growth.

As with any substantial structure its strength and durability is in its foundations, they underpin and support the building, equivalent to the deeply embedded roots of a tree that keep it sturdy, upright and strong. The depth of your belief infrastructure determines the firmness, power and stability of your belief construction and the dexterity of your bricks to stick together with formidable tenacity. Time, experience, determination, endurance and your outright boldness are all instrumental in the architecture of substantial belief foundations, the very fortification and resolve of your belief stronghold.

CHAPTER 3

Hope

'Without a single thought it battles through adversity, coercion and the jaundiced attitudes of others and mercilessly evades our own counteractive and sometimes inherent blindness.'

The premonition was vivid, an uneasy apprehensive state of mind, nothing visual just an internal disquiet, which just wasn't strong enough to change my stubborn set agenda for the day. It was intuition but years before I completely understood the powerful force of the inner voice. As the three men approached, I could almost read their minds, I was able to visualise in graphic motion, it suddenly all made perfect sense, in those split seconds before impact the fretfulness and anxiety I'd randomly experienced only hours ago was clearly trying to persuade a change in my plans and avoid the vicious assault about to happen. *'I told you so, I told you so, I told you so'* my subconscious mind screamed at me in synchronised unison with each hefty blow that mercilessly reigned upon my head, I was bludgeoned senseless for my briefcase, my wallet, a strip of blackcurrant flavoured chewing gum and a train ticket. Left unconscious and bleeding profusely I woke three hours later in a hospital as a nurse tried to determine who I was, I gave my name as each word I rendered callously discharged a searing ache into my severely concussed skull. My aching discomfort, disbelief and mental torture paled into insignificance compared to the horrific and shocking realisation I couldn't actually see the nurse I was agonisingly conversing with. I was blind. The relentless, crazed attack had affected my sight. They had barbarically and without pity taken my belongings and my vision.

Throughout my life I had pondered the misery of blindness that it would be incomprehensible not being able to see the beauty of the world, it had dawned upon me many times that losing one's sight was the ultimate torture God could bestow on someone because in their darkness they would still have the goading memories and images of everything they once saw and the stark comprehension of how they took for granted their amazing sense of vision. My inherent fear was now my depressing reality, the very unspeakable torture that once disturbed me, in a ghoulish twist of fate, was now bequeathed to me.

The diagnosis was desperate and vague, they didn't have a clue whether my sight would ever return, they couldn't make a direct connection to the assault and deemed the possibility it could be psychological blindness caused by extreme trauma. The term 'Hysterical Blindness' was being apathetically bandied around by the specialists, they were suggesting only psychiatry might be the cure, the shock and traumatisation of my ordeal had basically switched my eyes off, in exactly the same way you flick a light switch and turn the lights off, except in this case the switch was lost in the murky, hazy depths of my tortured mind. It was mental upheaval of the most bizarre, unlikely and cruel kind. Hours turned into days, days seemed an eternity without all the sights, colours and allure of the world we all take for granted. A world I couldn't see wasn't a world I wanted to be alive in, the only life I knew was one I could see, one I knew so well until only a handful of days ago. I was wilfully wishing my pathetic blind existence away. I passionately wanted to die. I used every moment of waking consciousness to curse a lengthy and tortuous death upon the perpetrators of my affliction. I imagined how I would slowly gouge their eyes out with a screwdriver, just so they could experience what they had harshly inflicted upon me.

A cold bleak, heartless bitterness that only invented harmful methods of administering pain upon others had replaced my confident and unmistakable positive outlook on life. A creature of disdain and rancid hatred, I despised the world that was no longer mine to see, how dare the earth revolved whilst mine had come to a grinding halt. I wished for the sun to burn out and become a black-hole in the sky, if I couldn't see it rise, it shouldn't be there at all, I wanted the entire world to be in pitch darkness. I spat venom at my visitors who dared to utter feeble, useless statements such as 'don't worry', 'it'll all be ok', 'you need to smile more'. Through my grimacing, unbeknown to them, there was a sinister smile, that simply hankered for people who uttered such nonsensical rubbish to die in horrific car crashes on their way home, or that they would just miraculously lose their sight, so I could say pathetic and meaningless things to them like 'don't worry just smile'. I was beginning to hate people, the world and more than anything else, my miserable self.

In three short but eternally long weeks I had been transformed into a cantankerous, self-pitying monster, my bitterness was borderline evil. I was falling deeper and deeper into a bottom-less and deathly pit of anger, despair and depression. Every waking day I cried uncontrollably through my useless eyes as I awoke and relentlessly begged God to have an ounce of pity and relieve me of the pointless and dark life I was leading.

'Without hope the heart truly dies', it was unusual to hear a friendly voice after all I'd banned most visitors and considering the rudeness and vitriol I fiercely showered upon anyone that dared to speak to me, the doctors & nurses had been reduced to uttering no more than obligatory pleasantries. Unusually my response was almost pleasant albeit my underlying sentiments still understandably bitter *'I'd rather die because I have no hope, my hope died the day my eyes did, I don't have anything to live for'.*

What the nurse said next, in a flash of inspiration changed my attitude and view on my inconsequential and futile life.

'Deep, deep inside your heart you have to believe you will see again. Even if you only have one tiny ounce of hope left that one day your sight will return, then you need to hang onto that because that one ounce of hope will get you through, that single ounce will give you a reason to live. Sometimes all you need is hope.'

It was a lightning strike moment as a bolt of electricity shot through me and that dormant ounce of hope was reawakened and started to beat enthusiastically deep in my heart. This angelic nurse sent from heaven above had truly given me a wonderful fresh burst of life, even describing the scene from my hospital window that patiently awaited the inevitable return of my vision.

'The grass is damp and dewy green, littered with thousands of gorgeous reddish brown autumnal leaves, that delicately fall and waft to the ground from the huge overpowering oak tree right outside your window. Right next to the huge tree is a sprightly flowing brook, the sparkling water is cascading and trickling over the pebbles as it glistens in the bright shining winter sun.'

This was sheer poetry to me. I could actually visualise the grass, the leaves, the tree, the water, the pebbles and the shining sun. My personal hell of doom and gloom blackness had within minutes, been transferred to a scene that everyone else took for granted, I could finally, through my blindness see a ray of hope shining out from my own dejected heart. Every day the nurse would return at random and unexpected times and utter the same beautiful, divine blessed words:

'Deep, deep inside your heart you have to believe you will see again. Even if you only have one tiny ounce of hope left that one day your sight will return, then you need to hang onto that because that one ounce of hope will get you through, that

single ounce will give you a reason to live. Sometimes all you need is hope.'

And every time she would describe the same stunning autumn scene that was serenely waiting for me.

As each day passed my hope grew stronger along with my internal resolve and determination to actually see the sight right outside my own window, a sight that I could already visualise with devastating clarity.

On a daily basis the entirety of my existence now revolved around hearing the nurse's celestial comforting words. They sank into my brain and raced around like a feisty rollercoaster through my veins until every living, breathing, beating cell of my body had a sense of hope and vigour that my eyes would once again let in light and see the glorious waiting world, a far cry from the daily suicidal emotions I was experiencing the day before the nurse materialised. I was no longer the pathetically sullen creature praying for death instead I was wishing for eternal, glorious life.

With divine hope at the steering wheel of my heart, soul and mindset there was a distant light at the end of my personal dark tunnel and within that tiny slither of hopeful light, I could see possibility, such immense possibility that I was driven to create a mesmerising and exhausting list of objectives, aspirations and goals that I desperately wanted to achieve the very minute my eyes were switched on again, I whimsically named my list 'The Hope, Vision & Possibility list' I was convinced that the majority of people, just like I was, were blind to possibility, despite having the omnipotent sense of vision. I'd never in my entire life had witnessed such crystal clear hope and vision and yet ironically I hadn't seen a flicker of light for weeks, I'd even forgotten the sight of my own grotty face. My blindness had given birth to unimaginable eyesight, perception and belief. Does one really have to be blind before they see the light, the blinding light of hope & possibility? That was certainly the case where I was concerned! My utter sullen hatred of the world had metamorphosed into complete gratitude for every breath I'd had, was currently taking and still had left in my sightless body.

Even my dreams had been transformed from nightmarish images of hell, fire-breathing demons, satanic rituals and death to visions of a bright and joyful world full of fun, laughter and happiness. In one particularly wonderful dream I awoke with my eyes painfully wide open as my restored vision let the sharp light in for the first time in eight long, dark weeks. I screamed at the top of my voice 'I can see, I can see, I can see', even though the laser-like brightness burnt through my retina, tears of ecstasy were flowing frantically down my face. This was the most welcome and amazing dream I'd ever dreamt, as three nurses and a doctor rushed to see what the commotion was, only to see me crying tears of joy and bellowing the same words over and over again 'I can see, I can see, I can see', they stood there in total excitable disbelief. Through the dreamy blurriness and haze of my barely open eyes I witnessed a breathtaking and poignant moment that became a landmark happening in my life, as they wept and applauded in sheer elation, I had the colossal and breathtaking realisation this wasn't a dream. I could actually see again. I was no longer blind.

Two months of unexpected blindness and the world was finally back, I was overcome with an erratic array of emotions from gratitude to incomprehensible excitement. Bizarrely my gratitude wasn't for the return of my sight, on the contrary it was for the fact that I'd seen the light through my blindness and the excitement was because I knew my returning vision was not the vision I'd originally lost but one of colossal possibility, expectation and enormous hope.

The hospital specialists were professionally stunned and wracking their medical brains. Unbeknown to me and according to their prognosis it was unlikely my sight would return for a few months yet, if at all. Their in-depth evaluation had concluded there were three combined causes of my unusual condition, obviously concussions to the skull, deep set emotional psychological trauma and existing chemical damage which may have been dormant until I'd received the violent blows to the head. They hadn't ascertained the cause of the latter, however it wasn't a mystery or surprise to me, as a tumultuous quantity of severe medicinal narcotics, diet suppressants and lethal weed killer had passed through my body and brain before I'd even left secondary school.

I explained to a team of doctors and a psychiatrist how one of the hospital nurses coaxed and encouraged a sense of hope within me and how that was the internal catalyst that sparked a powerful chain-reaction that ultimately spurred my vision to return. I even regaled them with the very sentence she lovingly whispered every day for weeks that instigated my mental recovery.

'Deep, deep inside your heart you have to believe you will see again. Even if you only have one tiny ounce of hope left that one day your sight will return, then you need to hang onto that because that one ounce of hope will get you through, that single ounce will give you a reason to live. Sometimes all you need is hope.'

They were touched by my emotional explanation and in total agreement that it would have been instrumental in aiding my staggering recovery, particularly in the absence of any medical theory they could conjure up. Naturally, I wanted to meet the angel that gave me that living, breathing vital ounce of hope, which entirely changed the course of my repugnant blind life and instilled into my tortured mind a greater vision than ever before, full of astonishing hope and mind-blowing possibility. I asked the ward Matron when my wonderful nurse would be on duty next. At that moment my romantic and fanciful anticipation of finally meeting the woman behind the soft, heavenly voice took a spooky and sinister twist, the Matron's haunting words left me bewildered and stunned into silence *'Michael, no nurse or Doctor has spoken to you for over a month now, they couldn't you were rude and repulsive. The only visitors you've had have been your family once or twice a week and they barely spoke to you, considering you'd banned them all from visiting you. Don't worry love you probably dreamt you were talking to a nurse.'* I spat venom at the Matron and called her an evil lying witch, demanding to see my nurse. The ward supervisor reluctantly came to my bedside, touched my hand and repeated almost word for word what the Matron had already shocked me with. There was no nurse there was no angel from above. I thought someone was mocking me surely this was a joke, somebody's idea of morose fun, a hugely unfunny sick joke. Then I remembered the stunning view from my window that had been affectionately described to me day after day, making me long to see it, such underestimated beauty just waiting for my eyes to indulge and appreciate it.

'The grass is damp and dewy green, littered with thousands of gorgeous reddish brown autumnal leaves, that delicately fall and waft to the ground from the huge overpowering oak tree right outside your window. Right next to the huge tree is a sprightly flowing brook, the sparkling water is cascading and trickling over the pebbles as it glistens in the bright shining winter sun.'

I leapt out of bed and trundled precariously over to the window, this was the first time in two months I'd seen my own feet take footsteps, it was a weird sensation to even see the floor I was walking on, I held the window ledge and stared out of the grubby window. My heart exploded with loathsome defeat as it was ripped from my ribcage and was callously thrown to the ground before being mercilessly squashed by the exceptionally heavy boot of reality. There was no oak tree, no grass, no brown autumnal leaves and no sprightly flowing brook, the only sight that confidently greeted me and ferociously slapped me in the face was an insipid tall, grey hospital tower block. Is this what a heart-attack felt like? There was a sharp, relentless pain in my chest, I was crestfallen, my emotions and thoughts were inconsolable as they tried to make sense of this bizarre debacle. I returned to my bed in a trance of utter confusion and lay there in irritated discontent.

Hope was the welcome culprit. It lurks in the depths of your mind just waiting for you to fall and when you do, when you're at the end of your tether, when all other god-given emotions have abandoned you, given you their worse bite and uncaringly walked away turning their back on you, all that remains is the black cloud of life that eagerly shrouds your existence and banishes the light you've always known, in those moments of complete shadowy desperation, a tiny shred of hope comes alive. Even when you feel you have absolutely no hope left, it still clears a path in the dark and dreary quagmire. A morning-dew size droplet of hope is strong and powerful enough to effectively confront your cruel bludgeoning enemies of defeat and battle through your barricades just to whisper the quietly deafening words in your ear *'don't give up'*, in my case the words that showered me with the all-seeing light were *'without hope the heart truly dies'*.

That single sentence pulled me through my dark days in hospital and still, to this very day remains a stern and commanding reminder of never giving up the battle. Each and every one of us has within our emotional artillery a fight called hope. A solitary insignificant murmur deep within our minds our real authoritative and prevailing back-bone, capable in an instance to stop a herd of angry elephants about to descend a trampling death upon us.

'Without hope the heart truly dies' was the title of a book I glanced upon a shelf years before my blindness and yet I had to actually go blind to discover it's true and poignant meaning, even though I'd never even read the contents. An immaterial book which undoubtedly cured my affliction and gave me absolute belief I would see the amazing view from my window. A view that didn't even exist but hope told me otherwise.

Is hope really that significant? Is it really that capable that it can procreate the bedrock of life itself? The answer is a resounding YES! The very hope of regaining my sight gave me an unparalleled vision and such immense possibilities that it even created an imaginary view from my window that urged and convinced my eyes to see again. Hope whispered, cried and screamed at me, it enabled me to believe I would have my sight back. It simply gave me BELIEF.

Within your bastion of belief is a staunch heartbeat breathing and pumping life into your belief bricks, keeping your stronghold cemented together, virile and strong. That heartbeat is hope, every second, of every hour, of every day feeding the pulse of life itself and sticking your belief bricks together.

The greater your hope the more unrelenting your belief, the more unrelenting and stalwart your belief is the greater your possibilities are.

I had sight but it was blindness that gave me hope, vision and possibility and in those reawakening dark days I unearthed a handful of inestimable strengths and almighty unquestionable guidelines that are predominant and can successfully command and steer the direction of our lives.

1. **HOPE** – Without it we cannot possibly survive, it feeds and fortifies belief and injects possibility into our lives 'Without hope the heart truly dies'. If there is nothing to hope for how can there be anything to live for? Hope will breathe eternal anticipation, confidence, faith and expectation into your life and unconditionally be the pillar that upholds every miniscule aspect of your existence. It may on occasions be considered no more than your day-dream, however never has there been such a powerful concept that can fuel and generate your heartbeat into your living perception and very reason you survive. Hope is the ceaseless, everlasting spring of water that nourishes the drought we're born into and quenches our thirsty lives with its immortal, inimitable force.

2. **VISION** – Wear a blindfold for a day (I wore mine for sixty long, dreary days and woke up appreciating all the things I took for granted).Through your blindfold be grateful for

the ability to see, however sight does not enable your vision. I was blind long before I actually went blind. I was wearing an invisible blindfold which restricted the sight of my possibilities, my future and my ability. Do you really see and understand the stupendous possibilities you're capable of? Hope gives you boundless vision and lights the path to all realms of possibility. Through my blindness I created a world that didn't exist and empowered my mind to cure my visual defect. That defect was more than just my sight it was my conceptualising and vision for the future. Your own vision is infinite, it has no limitable realm, its domain is the universe and beyond, its empire is far greater than your sight could ever be. On a daily basis vision, our ability to see further than our visual limits is attacked and sabotaged, clouding the immense kingdom of possibility we were born to see, imagine and reach. The antidote is hope, belief and that intimate curiosity and imagination that there is so much more in the world than our eyes deceive us to believe.

3. **POSSIBILITY** - Through my blindness I developed a consummate acknowledgement and indebtedness to life and the frighteningly stark realisation how utterly futile and insignificant my role in this short drama we're born into was. Void of dreams, aspirations and desire, a life of little consequence. I was merely surviving not living. Surely every character in their personalised stage show of life had the legitimate choice to take the leading role, to be the hero, the dominant protagonist, instead of settling for the role of an inconsequential extra, playing a part of the meaningless background, every day just watching the main actors playing their governing parts with complete gusto and achieving the applause, the rewards and the recognition they truly deserved. The principal character we're all born to play isn't contrived through nature neither is it nurture, it's plainly a matter of individual choice. Hope and vision opens the door to possibility and the attitude to

design and conduct the part you truly want to play in your own production of life. This monumental realisation whilst living my life in consummate darkness was the momentous flash of inspiration and light, sustained and powered by glorious hope, that gave the timely birth of my own 'Hope, Vision & Possibility' list. A simple top ten that I desperately wanted to achieve before I lost my sight again or worse, before my life ended. This was the true birth of possibility.

The cloud of desperation to accomplish my 'Hope, Vision and Possibility' list had been originated. Rather than creating unsightly shade it showers me with rainstorms of encouragement, enthusiasm and inspiration. It discharges pitiless lightning bolts that scathe and bombard procrastination with the dreadful fear and anticipation of failure. Deafening claps of thunder are customary and rudely awaken slumber in my dreaded comfort zone.

Any sincere, wholehearted and meaningful 'Hope, Vision and Possibility' list comes with the customary 'cloud of desperation', if it doesn't and you're not regularly showered, shot, inspired and cajoled into action then you honestly don't have a true understanding of your personal possibility or heartfelt desires. I've already achieved milestones on my list which entices new additions as life goes on, experiences widen and vision continues to develop, magnify and broaden. 'Motivation from a Tortured Mind' was one of the very first fundamental landmarks of possibility on my list. Writing a book wasn't simply an everyday goal, it was an impossibility made possible through hope and vision it was truly something I never thought I'd be capable of achieving in my minimal and grossly limited lifetime. A seedling that had been sown by an English Lecturer who wholeheartedly believed every individual has an unwritten book within them. The tragedy of life being they never put it into words.

Possibility is having the hope and vision to accomplish majestic, unforgettable, awe-inspiring achievements that stand alone as a fertile living, panting oasis in a barren desert of unimaginative, mediocre and habitual goals. They are borne of dreams, the things you conjure when you imagine without limits, with no boundaries, without even a plan of action. It's the magic of flawless, crystal clear, uninterrupted visualising. Only in those very magical and compelling dreams did I ever write a book, never daring to believe it could possibly become an everyday reality. Inadvertent hope through blindness created the visual images of possibility and mind-blowing dreams became sparkling, illuminating beacons lighting the path to 'Motivation from a Tortured Mind'. I pictured this book with clarity for years before I wrote a single word, from the cover to the quirky provocative and earnest title I saw it, just like I saw the view from my hospital window, it was there, living, breathing and existing. The vision of possibility got stronger and gathered vigorous momentum as each occurrence and life experience added to the pages of my dream. Each day, week and year that passed, put more words into place, a book that started as just hope, vision and possibility, with nothing more than a wacky title, gathered a ferocious snowballing pace, until finally an action plan and agenda materialised and created an active, once unimaginable reality.

Vicious lightning bolts and vociferous claps of thunder continued to transpire from the cloud of desperation that tracked and followed my every move. Not writing my book was strictly unquestionable and never an option or even a fleeting negative thought. The resounding fear of failure bludgeoned my writing goal into submission with a heavy, blunt instrument called success. I was obsessively desperate to achieve this vision. Every book I saw on every bookshelf, in every home, shop and library, shouted, screeched and hollered panic into my already impetuous and tortured mind. On a repetitive and daily basis my brain hurriedly accumulated more and more information and direction, turning everyday life into words and pages of motivation. It had no choice the lightning bolts were getting swifter and more savage turning the contagion of procrastination into smouldering, dying embers. The debilitating comfort zone that plagues all of us had no resting place as the boom of thunder scared it into petrified oblivion. Desperation was the desirable motivation constructing a dream.

It begins with impassioned hope, which propagates laser-like vision, such mental perception proliferates the contingency of possibility. In the valuable and breathtaking predicament of believing dreams are acutely attainable the desire and desperation to achieve otherwise inconceivable life-changing conquests is uncompromising and relentless. Without a single thought it battles through adversity, coercion and the jaundiced attitudes of others and mercilessly evades our own counteractive and sometimes inherent blindness.

CHAPTER 4

Desperation

'The desperate frame of mind can create untold mental pandemonium and yet become the catalyst for immeasurable achievements, propagating success, challenging perception and changing the course of our entire lives.'

When faced with an abhorrent situation alien to our everyday lives our rationale changes and challenges our inherent learning and we react in ways that are usually conflicting to our personal characteristics. We may take actions that otherwise may not have even occurred to us, actions that are based on essential need, not the exclusivity of choice.

The feeling of complete desperation can have numerous causes and can bring about a whole plethora of emotions ranging from anxiety, concern, dejection, agony, despair, distress to outright doom and gloom. Already throughout this book you have physically & mentally identified with certain emotions and reacted based on your own life experiences and elementary culture. Desperation will be one of those emotions. The degree to which you have associated with it is purely proportional to the benchmark of desperation you've already experienced in your life. For example anyone that has been unfortunate enough to temporarily lose their sight will exclusively relate to my blindness episode and fully recognise the deluge of emotions I suffered. If you've never experienced such an adverse affliction then your reaction to my grief will be governed by your imagination and trying to imagine what losing your vision would feel like. This process of adapting your mind heightens your apprehension and understanding of scenarios and ultimately allows you to examine, comprehend, evolve and regenerate your philosophy & thinking. Fundamentally the result will be an improvement in your personal development through your innate aptitude to greatly evolve the emotions that are consistent with the positive attitude vital for mental growth. You've already demonstrated this mental metamorphosis and acumen when you succinctly thought about the dysfunctional firework, not only because you've had an avalanche of dissatisfied situations throughout your life but also because you were consciously able to connect happenings in your life with that metaphorical example.

Whether you own or rent your home, it's your home. It's your place of solace, the place that comforts you, fills you with contentment, your bed of roses, your escape, your castle, your defence from the world. It's the roof over your head, your most cherished belonging. It's the one possession that's worth the most both financially and physically. Even the mention of the word 'home', fills most people with warmth, tranquillity & safety. I'm certain unless you're actually homeless (in which case if you're reading this book, you're either searching for a solution to your misery or you haven't quite comprehended your dire circumstances), that for most of you these are precisely the pleasant and stable emotions running through your mind.

Imagine the scenario your life is put into turmoil because you're given three months notice on the repossession of your home. I want you to put yourself directly into that situation. Wherever you live, whatever your home looks like, you're now going to lose it. Everything you've worked for, everything you're worth, everything you know, appreciate & cherish will be callously and without a second thought will be snatched from you.

You are literally helpless to halt this unexpected downslide in your life. In exactly three months you will be homeless, all that resides in your mind is the hair-raising vision that you'll be forced into being one of those begging vagabonds that irritatingly get in your way, that are no more than a nuisance in your hurried, scuttling life, an inconvenience on the pavement, an annoyance in your path. You will be that plague on the landscape of society, begging passers-by for a living.

It's probably a gross understatement to describe your frame of mind as desperate. You're feeling pathetic, abandoned, vulnerable & destitute, probably with a substantial dose of anger, fear and exasperation thrown in for good measure. This is how I want you to feel when I mention 'desperate'. There are certain emotions such as the ones just described that are pivotal to our development and growth and in reality have been the essential and integral mental assault many people needed, to force and stimulate their lives into the direction of their dreams.

If you're just not buying into the 'home' dilemma and not quite feeling the emotions I've listed above, let's try and agitate you with an alternative synopsis. How about your job, it's how you survive, it pays for the things you want, the roof over your head (the one you can't imagine being without), the food on the table, the clothes you wear, the entertainment and luxuries you partake in. In most cases the entire sustenance and survival of your family. It's clearly the foundation of the life you have, including the acquaintance and familiarity of having a daily function, something to be a part of something that not only sustains you but gives you that sense of secure belonging.

It's now three weeks before Christmas, the accustomed celebrations are already setting in. The mood is changing as the spirit of 'good-will to all men' that we're conditioned with from an early age is predictably and charmingly washing over everyone. There is affection, humour and tomfoolery in the usually stale office air. Individuals possess a different aura with all their doldrums and petty issues appropriately pushed aside in your now sparkling Christmassy workplace. The decorations, even though they are past their shelf life, have been dragged out kicking and screaming, for another year to create the glittery grotto you now work in, someone even dons a pathetic Santa hat but it's all enjoyably acceptable at this time of year. All is complacent and smug in the world with the anticipation of the forthcoming frivolity and jubilation. People are talking about their plans for the season, the shopping, the presents, the hullabaloo, the seasonal merriment. The splurge of parties and shindigs has already begun, with revellers regaling each other with feats of drinking excessive alcohol and the resulting drunken horseplay. The annual office party is looming with its very own serving of delightful foolishness, expected irresponsibility and sweeping giddiness. Television is awash with jolly, audacious advertising selling you everything from luxurious presents to amazing toys and delectable, mouth-watering food & drink. Once again Christmas has crept up on you but is most welcome and as with every year since you were old enough to recognise it, ardently captures your imagination and brings about the comfort & joy associated with this celebratory and convivial time of year. There is a cold, snowy crispness in the air as the winter season takes an icy grip on the world but it matters not one jot, it's what makes December magical and endearing. The lights are twinkling in the shops and the town centres are a jolly change from the usual grubby, congested mess. Christmas is certainly all around which includes the glowing, cheerful anticipation and warming blanket of optimism in your head.

Now here's the unexpected crunch, it's a normal Friday at work and as is regularly the weekly scenario, like clock-work you're summoned into your Manager's office. Undoubtedly it'll be the usual inconsequential banter, just his uneducated take on leadership, a few absurd and predictable words to exercise his insignificant power and self-satisfied status. Well, at least it makes him feel good and if he feels good life is much easier.

Nevertheless his normal aimless expression is replaced with a grizzled, weary grimace, it's either chronic constipation or he is troubled, either way its causing an unlikely and awkward atmosphere, which is further aggravated by his lack of eye contact.

Then unexpectedly and like a power drill piercing your brain, come the fatal opening words that usually signify your fate is doomed, no matter who spouts the killer sentence 'There's no easy way of saying this...' In that split second, that seems to last a lifetime and seems like hours before the next words are muttered, your mind has taken a negative quantum leap. Your ability of visualisation is suddenly crystal clear and has just improved one hundred fold transporting you to the misery, sadness and grief of unpaid mortgages, unfulfilled promises and a planned holiday that has just violently unplanned itself, with you, cap in hand stood in the queue at the benefits office with all the other unemployed people, who all probably had to endure the same killer sentence. All that in a second of hearing those desperate words 'There's no easy way of saying this...' Nevertheless, there's an ounce of hope deep within you, which defies your painfully dying heart and eases your tortured mind full of adverse thoughts and associated numbness.

That miniscule dash of hope is insensitively crushed, a poison arrow shoots straight through your heart, doom and destiny has weaved its evil web and is confirmed and compounded by the rest of the sentence '...so I'll tell you straight, we're going to have to let you go'.

Three weeks before Christmas your world of predictable festive glory has come crashing down to your ankles. From joyful, seasonal excitement and anticipation, Christmas has with the breath of one damning sentence, turned to a scornful tasteless infliction. You walk out of your Manager's office a broken person, destitute, impoverished and drained of all good-will. Your mind is racing from one poverty-stricken thought to another. Your plans, your aims, your arrangements have all been squashed like a meaningless insect, who's loss means absolutely bugger-all to the world but has disappeared like yours, in a flash callously transformed into a dark void of nothingness. The big, ugly corporate boot has given you just that, the boot. You are now purposeless, diminutive and irrelevant. Your official corporation superiority has been stripped and apathetically pushed into a dark, deep well where it has perished, drowning in cold and murky water. That flea-infested beggar you irreverently stepped over on your way into work this morning, like he was a deformed, inconvenient monstrosity is no longer the scourge of society. Your perception of life has been tragically altered. He is now a poor down-trodden casualty of the bastard system that controls this corrupt world, suddenly you have something in common with a tramp you barely noticed just a few hours before. Both of you now have a vulnerable and unstable future with a mindset and heart struggling to find hope.

Undoubtedly, if you've never yet understood desperation then these two likely and every day scenarios of potentially losing your home or your job may just spark, within you, emotions associated with feeling desperate.

The powerhouse emotion of desperation is capable of moving mountains and parting the most virile sea, it can categorically shift people into actions and mental astuteness that otherwise may have eluded them and their normal ability. Desperate people do desperate things. A tortured mind will be twice as industrious to placate such a hopelessly futile and inconsolable mindset as one that isn't experiencing discomfort.

My, exclusive foresight and subjective outlook into the unenthused domain of having a desperate philosophy materialised with an almighty and totally unexpected crash, bang, wallop and earth-shattering shudder. Destiny had steered both disastrous situations of losing my job and my home directly to my doorstep. A doorstep, that with the rest of my house was merely three months away from repossession and was a direct consequence of losing my job three weeks before Christmas, with those fatalistic, damning un-enigmatic words *'There's no easy way of saying this...'.*

Aside from all the obvious emotions I went through, it was being awkwardly plunged headfirst into a do or die situation that was most alarming. If there ever was an opportunity to lie down and accept defeat then this was it, all the odds were acutely stacked against me. However, the change this forced upon me was far greater than losing my job and my home, the change was simply the power of desperation, the alteration in perception it brings and the understanding it's the only and closest match to the unequivocal power and capability of fear itself.

The consequences of my personal gloomy and deplorable circumstances were outstanding in terms of achievement, personal development and mental attitude. The fear of loss that had been thrust upon me withstood every conceivable challenge and obstacle that dared to obstruct my journey through the dark tunnel I was in. There was only one route and one direction it was simply fast-forward at immense break-neck speed, rapidly crushing anything that stood in my way. Otherwise mandatory sleeping and eating became optional, as fear staved off tiredness and fuelled my hunger. The deadline for my goals had been firmly set by an outside force. It was three very short months, in which time-line the mortgage lenders were going to take back what was rightfully theirs, my home. In those testing ninety days with the cloud of desperation and fear hanging over me, through sheer dogged determination, consistent effort and a sharp concentrated mental image of once again being secure in my job and living without the harassing fear of a repossession knock on the door, I did everything within my grasp and extensively outside of my dreaded comfort zone to create income and procure a substantial and distinguished job. Consequently the new position of employment was far superior to the one I had been forced out of, the aftermath of which was not only holding onto my home but actually buying a better one at twice the price in an exceptional neighbourhood.

This episode of fear and desperation wasn't about achievement, determination or even learning that success is readily available once you step outside of your comfort zone and treat the luxury of sleeping and eating as optional. It was far greater than those obvious and likely assumptions. The most thought provoking attribute of those three months was I had circumnavigated my life to a wonderful new home, an amazing new career and a lifestyle far more abundant and remarkable than ever before, however none of my supplementary and desirable life would have materialised had I not heard those baneful and dreaded seven words 'There's no easy way of saying this....' In other words, I wouldn't have my newfound luxury had I not been pitilessly fired. I was content with an average job, a standard home and a humdrum lifestyle. I never imagined I would have ever thanked my previous boss for coldly and swiftly firing me three weeks before Christmas (just so you know, for that hugely therapeutic and rewarding sense of personal gratification I did exactly that, I thanked him personally for being integral in my huge positive shift in life). I had never envisaged an alternative existence than the average ignorance I was living, until I had no choice. It was the elimination of that choice that compelled the changes I made without any procrastination.

Circumstance was clearly my provocation and ultimately my motivator but how does one achieve such accomplishments naturally, without disaster and fear fuelled incitement being the instigators?

The power of desperation and its awe-inspiring ability to drive people to success has always intrigued me, particularly when a close friend who normally couldn't scrape enough cash to watch a film at the cinema or have the everyday luxury of a take-away meal, managed to raise thirty thousand pounds in less than four months.

How did someone who was a self-confessed sponge of the state that couldn't be bothered to follow through with an education or any form of career manage such an incredible

Motivation from a Tortured Mind

feat? The culprit was pure, unadulterated desperation. His reasons changed and left him void of choice, no longer could he choose to live a lackadaisical, unaffected life, there was only one way forward. It wasn't nature or nurture that pushed the monumental shift in his attitude it was irreproachable choice, borne of having the luxury of free-will violently and callously removed from his being.

The very reason his world revolved, the essence, soul & sparkle of everything he lived for had been threatened with death.

The utterly unthinkable had become his reality.

His very reason for living, his joy, laughter & celebration, his sheer meaning in life & fulfilment was threatened. Not physically by another but by a questionable twist in fate, a perilous act of God. His only child that had been forced to live a below average life was plummeted into a treacherous and life threatening situation. It was a cancerous sickness. Aggressive, painful, insufferable, deplorable, it affected his parents to their very core with a detestable and intolerable inner pain. The fear of loss was uncontrollable and unstoppable but so was the almighty quest to raise money for a revolutionary procedure only available in Switzerland, a procedure that could signal the difference between life and death.

Without a single contradictory thought their very beliefs, propriety and attitude to almost everything in their existence was force fed into a huge unforgiving meat grinder. Everything they knew and understood was mercilessly crushed, mangled and destroyed to create an entirely new universe, that was honed into the quandary of finding ways that could achieve the normality they once took for granted, a quandary that had a hefty price tag of thirty thousand pounds and an even heftier price tag if they were unsuccessful in their mission. They experienced every detrimental emotion known to mankind from agony, anguish, misery, torture, grief to utter despair all of which collectively and unanimously forced and engineered a state of DESPERATION.

One by one the mental shackles that had restricted growth, success and development within my friend were shattered, by an apathetic and emotionless sledgehammer called 'Fear'. That desperate fearless hammering to his soul recognised no challenge, obstruction or hurdle in the pursuit of accomplishment. The reward of such relentless action and attitude was the perseverance of life itself. Thirty thousand pounds had saved their son from an early exit and slaughtered the fear that they would outlive their only offspring, in a miserable life of regret and immense sadness.

Desperation is a powerful force. It's the overpowering feeling of loss itself, the fear of losing, a sense of uncontrollable deprivation from the very things we live with, adore and rely on. The accidental or inadvertent failure to hold onto something physical or something perceived. The recklessness of despair caused by a fear you're going to lose an article, commodity, belonging or emotional attachment.

Desperation is the mental turmoil and agitation caused by the renunciation, denial and cancellation of opportunity, achievability, prospects, perception and potential. It's the loss of hope, of being hopeless and physically or mentally being unable to deal with the situation. It is succinctly described as a state of despair and yet it can breed gargantuan shifts in perception and human possibility, creating and forcing feats of unimaginable greatness.

The desperate frame of mind can create untold mental pandemonium and yet become the catalyst for immeasurable achievements, propagating success, challenging perception and changing the course of our entire lives.

Imagine the possibility if we could harness such power to generate success and do it without the prequel of desperation.

1. In reality we lead exceptionally desperate lives. The burgeoning cloud of desperate inevitability follows us everywhere. Our lives are limited our existence is rented

floor-space. Our landlord with an acute sense of randomness decides when he wants his earthly floor-space back and then with total inflexibility and hardhearted impertinence retrieves it for someone else to have, abandoning us to the graveyard of history and has-beens. What's the difference between that impending doom to being actually told you only have months to live, or you're being made redundant, or you're losing your home or worse still someone you dearly love is terminally ill? The answer is nothing, there is no difference except the mountainous handicap of our own thinking and mental agility. Every tick of the clock, every precious moment that passes us by is predictably another notch on our landlord's gloomy timescale. Somewhere in his official unearthly residence he's counting down to our demise, your epitaph is already written and your gravestone engraved. The words on both are what you've created and designed already and emblazoned your life with. That is a fact, there is no changing it, exploring it, escaping it, or tricking it and the only modicum of vital information that eludes us, is how much time we were granted on our personal time-scale of desperate life. Each day we shirk the responsibility of paying our landlord the rent for being alive, therefore every day is another uncanny escape from the jaws of death and desperation, every day should be an acknowledgement, an indebtedness to being animatedly existent and yet sometimes our gratitude is complacent and we wholeheartedly accept what we have and strive for no more.

2. Living a life of forced desperation is unnecessary, considering the majority of associated emotions are mentally cumbersome and undesirable. However, treating each segment of our lives with an element of fateful, binding closure may just create the necessary mental momentum associated with not possessing the luxury of choice. It's that very luxury we're nonchalantly handed that slows down our progress and limits our potential. My life would

not have moved on had it not been for those fateful words linked to losing my job and home. Once the demon known as 'choice' was vigorously removed, my life moved onto a level that I never knew existed. Choice had metaphorically made me blind to possibility and availability. The removal of that choice gave my life an energetic vigour I'd seldom experienced and yet that very success that I accomplished was there for the taking long before I was hammered with desperation.

3. Think, imagine and evolve without the power of choice which respectfully can almost hold you back in your crusade for abundance. Every life has greater potential than is imaginable, every life currently being lived has within it a far greater purpose and existence. Sometimes we can't visualise such beauty and prospects until the clouds of desperation pour destructive rain upon our lives. Hazardous downpours are a reality but they can also create an ending, an ending that has no light at the end of the tunnel. Long before the heavens open and shower you with inevitability and heinous desperation, realise and contemplate the worse case scenarios and from those possible torrential downpours, imagine what you can do to make the differences you crave. The very differences and accomplishments that desperation pressures you into achieving by the abolishment of choice and judgement. Let the onslaught of imminent desperation fulfil your life with commanding and potent desire.

CHAPTER 5

Desire

'If you can harness the dynamism, compulsion, stimulus and potency of desire there is nothing in the realms of victory and accomplishment that you can't achieve.'

A furiously pounding and quickening heartbeat, relentless, frenzied, uncontrollably fast, sensationally beating out of your chest. An increase in temperature, bodily heat and sweating, bringing on feverish burning sensations. Mental distracted agitation, impatient and irregular thoughts many of them frantic, nervous, erratic and eccentric, a dreamy wistful forlorn disposition levelling somewhere between reality and fantasy. All the heady symptoms of a fateful tropical disease spreading its viral destruction, through an unwelcoming human body, undoubtedly causing the casualty an unnecessary amount of sickness and unrelenting pain. On the other hand it can be physically sexual, cerebrally seductive, brilliantly bewitching, intensely alluring or severely tempting, that's the overpowering condition and feeling known as desire.

Wanting, craving, longing, yearning for something so bad it almost makes your body, mind & soul unrecognisable from your normal day-to-day character. Akin to a surreal affliction, irritation and sickness that categorically refuses to subside, until it's nourished with whatever metaphorical medicine it's aching for.

It encourages your appetite, increases your hunger, exacerbates your motive, strengthens your purpose, fuels your compulsion, boosts your need, powers your passion, heightens your infatuation and provokes your propensity to achieve success. If there ever was a cornerstone & fundamental requirement to achievement above all ability, skill, knowledge, experience or education it's the consciousness and harnessing of desire.

Desire alone can fuel, force and motivate an adequate quantity of mental stimuli and ferocious determination within every human-being and fuel their journey to accomplish whatever they want.

It finds a way. It'll show you a path that otherwise may have eluded you. It'll plan, decide and create subconscious action for you, followed by an aptitude to achieve. It'll map your mind with clarity, understanding & vigour. It'll diminish doubt, peter out indecision and lengthen your resolve. It's the highest rated power-tool available to mankind, gargantuan in size & dexterity and capable of tackling any stipulation, extremity, compulsion and obstacle that has the audacity of being in your way.

Conversely, it can conjure totally delirious, foolish, incoherent and irrational behaviour, rarely associated with sanity & intelligence. Antithetical to creating a force of positive conquest, the dynamism of desire by sheer nature of its inability to be a rational form of thinking has the innate capability of complete and utter warfare and undesirable havoc.

The Fire

The fierce flames were unified in their mission as they lapped at the walls with a lavish and coordinated irreverence. Rapidly and without hesitation spreading their evil destruction and carnage to anything that dared to be in their unfortunate path.

If the antique clock on the wall could have recorded the exact time the fire began, it would only have ticked another four minutes, it's glass face now saddened with cracks as the fire devilishly reflected it's destruction. Within those short minutes the thick golden, velvety floor to ceiling curtains were part of the disastrous carnival of fire, they were aiding and abetting its inglorious rise to new levels. It had already reached the ceiling and was eating away like a million hungry locusts on an unsuspecting corn-field full of ripe food. Except, locusts don't devour human flesh, unlike this bloodthirsty, murderous monster, intent on causing maximum harm without an ounce of discretion to all inanimate objects and human-beings.

With no respect for its masters, the very beings that usually control it, like a crazed demon, it was devouring inch by inch, everything in its calamitous path. It raced across the mantelpiece shelf, almost stopping to fiendishly laugh at the family in the framed photograph, before reducing the parents, daughter of eighteen years and twin ten year old boys to a smouldering, pile of memories, just indiscriminately wiped away.

It was almost as if the destruction of the picture gave the bellowing flames another evil idea. Suddenly, its intensity, heat and smoke doubled with glee. The family were all asleep upstairs and this merciless fire wasn't about to accept anything less than murder. It blew, seething, vitriolic toxic smoke through every frame, crack and crevice it could find. Like an inverted avalanche the torrent of fumes ascended upwards to greet the slumbering, innocent beings. Callously with untold cowardice knowing who to attack first, the youngest and the most innocent had their tiny lungs filled to poisonous capacity. Showing the only compassion it could, the black, poisonous fumes stole their short, incomplete, angelic lives without a murmur. The twins didn't even acknowledge the destruction, whisked away with the same expressions they fell asleep with, those of contentment and childish happiness. The last ever bedtime story they heard, being the final words to enter and gratify their tiny, unfulfilled minds. The very same person that so lovingly read those words couldn't save them from their melancholy goodbye to a world that only kept them alive for ten measly years.

The walk-by hero was just too late, he kicked his way into the house but the inferno was far too intelligent, nimble and calculating. Where the flames couldn't command the elimination of life, the smoke was leading the way and was victorious in that one-sided pointless but heroic battle. He couldn't even climb the stairs and was maliciously subjected to their screams, cries and pain as they met their fate. The fire-brigade arrived, the only artillery any match for the might of the deathly force and finally with a reluctant salute, it showed some reverence and threw in the towel.

Through the smouldering remains came the macabre reality, caused by sixty minutes of unsolicited fiery mayhem. The twins untouched by the fire were ironically the lucky ones, their lives furtively snatched without any pain. There was no mercy for the Mother, cremated in the bedroom, into an unrecognisable heap of tragic, skeletal human remains. The father and daughter were the only survivors, no longer recognisable, donning the scars and suffering of ninety percent burns. Their personal ordeals paled into insignificance with the emotional torment and suffering of their loss. Both wishing and praying that death had also paid them a swift visit.

The earth shattering headline that shook the community, the town and the entire Country was *'Boyfriend overcome by DESIRE, causes family tragedy'.*

Our pre-meditated walk-by hero, a normal, well-adjusted man of eighteen, showing absolutely no post event mental issues, had set the house alight and caused the unnecessary deaths and carnage and was my first real, emotive introduction to the powerful bulldozing effect of desire.

Irrational, absurd and wholly unreasonable actions as a result of one authoritative and convincing emotion, which I found extremely difficult to rationalise. How could desire be so hypnotically powerful that it could persuade a perfectly sane person to carry out such predetermined insanity resulting in the murder of innocent people?

In his own words blind with desire he turned to pyromania. He contrived the situation of setting their house alight and expected to heroically jump in and save the family and consequently win back the affections of the daughter, his ex-girlfriend. Their relationship had sourly ended, partly to the disapproving father, who thought he just wasn't good enough for his only daughter. He wanted to be the desirable hero who saved the family from perishing and become irresistible to his estranged lover and establish the approval of her reluctant father, the two people he subsequently destroyed physically and mentally. This demonstrates the foolish and uncontrollable power and force of desire. It's the one emotion that sparks huge, unbelievable achievements but one that can almost control our very existence.

If you can harness the dynamism, compulsion, stimulus and potency of desire there is nothing in the realms of victory and accomplishment that you can't achieve. Understanding your personal desire is the one single-most, important and valuable triumph you can ever undertake. One that will undoubtedly change your existence beyond any recognition. It's the primary principal of shifting life into fast-forward mode, the beginning of your greatest and most poignant journey.

Delicious Toffee Fudge

My phone was ringing incessantly, I didn't answer it. It was my colleague updating the status of his very slow and laborious motorway journey. He was at a standstill in ten solid miles of bumper to bumper cars. We were racing to the same meeting, except I was about ten miles or so ahead of him.

'No doubt you're on the phone, I'm stuck in a long queue, just heard on the radio there's been an accident and the

motorway is temporarily shut as they clear the wreckage, was just wondering where you've got to, I bet you just missed it, typical!'

That was followed by another message a few moments later.

'Just heard some poor bastard is trapped in his car, it's upside down on its goddamn roof! How on earth does anyone manage to do that, anyway the motorway will stay closed for another half an hour while they rescue the fool.'

How does a car end up on its roof? Quite easily really!

I hadn't answered my phone because I couldn't. Why? Because, I was that 'poor bastard' trapped in my car which was perched upside down and holding up hundreds of cars, as each very slowly passing driver asked themselves the very same question 'how does a car end up on its roof?' It was caused by a split second of lethal distraction while I fumbled around for another delicious fudge toffee, at that moment in time the desire to eat a tasty sweet was far greater than the massive risk of taking my eyes off the road. At considerable speed my car swerved onto the inclined grassy verge and judging by the position it stopped in, must have literally taken off, acrobatically turning due to the speed and launching incline and to the utter amazement of anyone watching crashed and crunched onto its roof, trapping the said 'fool' firmly within it. There I was in my delirious topsy-turvy situation covered in blood and vomit and still void of a delicious fudge toffee.

In the fifty one minutes it took between the 'delicious toffee fudge' accident happening and being loaded onto an ambulance, every emotion known to mankind, including a few reserved for obscure situations as these went through my luckily and bizarrely still alive mind. Hysterical thoughts ranged from the absurd and bewildering to thought provoking, life changing epiphanies.

'Why on earth did this have to happen the day I'm wearing my pale cream suit.'

'I wish I could answer that bloody phone.'

'I wonder if I'm already dead. I should make a list of all those I'm going to haunt at least I'm wearing my favourite pale cream suit because undoubtedly this is the one I'll always wear now that I'm a ghost, I'm stuck with it. At least its dapper, I could have died naked.'

'All this carnage for a delicious toffee fudge that I still want but just cannot reach.'

And *'Do I look like I'm alright you idiot?'* which was what I thought after the first driver on the scene nervously asked the laughable question *'are you alright?'*

Outside my vice versa caged hell was tumultuous and noisy activity. I wasn't hurt but it didn't look that way, I'm literally on my head covered in blood which was only because I'd bitten into my lip but it looked acutely dramatic spread all over my face, particularly as it drenched my once pristine favourite pale cream suit into a sickly deep crimson ugly mess. I'd created mass hysteria by simply wanting a delicious fudge toffee. Fifty one minutes of live, heart-stopping entertainment not forgetting ten miles of cursing drivers all now late for their destinations.

I was stuck in my own personal episode of extreme desperation and drama. I couldn't physically do a thing. The crash landing had wrapped me in a straight-jacket of bent, twisted metal and broken glass and a debilitating mental cocoon. Both my restricting physical surroundings plus emotional shock had rendered all my limbs absolutely useless, they had come to a grinding halt, much like the effect I'd had on the traffic. Fifty one minutes that actually seemed like a lifetime of lying still in this bizarre, visually stunning, breathtaking car wreck. A plethora of anxious scurrying emergency services and random people just looking in at me as if they were patiently waiting for the caged monkey to perform, intermittently tapping on the car to keep my attention, just in case my heart or my brain were in the departure lounge about to leave my body for good. Finally, after what seemed like days, they delicately and very cautiously dragged me out of the smoking, bloody tangle and tended to my horrendous but easily treatable bleeding lip, their facial expressions suggesting 'is that it?', poking and prodding my body trying to locate more striking physical damage. Clearly there was a certain amount of disbelief and naturally surprised relief as the unpleasant sight of the wreckage insinuated a myriad of sinister and ghastly injuries, far greater than a bleeding lip. In my mind I was almost apologising to the voyeuristic crowd that there weren't any mutilated limbs to physically and emotionally sicken my rescuers and spectators, I was sorry to let them down with such a crash, the least I could have provided was a live roadside amputation. The hasty and considerate rescue obliterated the disturbing illusions and cackling sounds my tortured mind was callously and rapidly reawakening, namely three absurdly grotesque witches that were flying through the haze of the crash, a deeply penetrating reminder of dormant and acutely neurotic childhood memories.

Beyond the emotional extremities and vivid apparitions I experienced during those shocking fifty one minutes, I also encountered a renewed focus. It was a sharp intake of desire in the most unlikely situation, both desire of romantic proportions, the human demand to fulfil our base necessities and the need to increase my materialistic collateral.

Once again this miserly shred of existence we refer to as 'life' was desperately hanging in the balance, precariously teetering in the void between living and dying, in the split second it took for my car to acrobatically somersault through the air visions of personal success and failure flashed through my labyrinthine imagination, images and expressions of highs and lows, of exaggerated laughter and bitter tears. The bone crunching crash, bang wallop as my car reconnected with the motorway tarmac, literally brought me crashing back to earth and my thoughts to survival mode. However, on this occasion my inbuilt danger barometer had already indicated this latest bout of bawdy shenanigans was not of the life threatening variety, possibly because my afflicted mind had already been inoculated against such capers. My demeanour had developed an indifference to such physical and mental torture having encountered numerous mischievous happenings in my life. This escapade was just another heart-stopping, car turning, blood spurting, joint dislocating situation.

The delicious fudge toffee happening wasn't necessarily a classic epiphany of life-altering consequences, it was further understanding of how the power and emotions of desperation can unleash our otherwise limited ability to see beyond what is currently in our hands. Yet another clarification of what we can truly achieve if only we could open our eyes widely and realise our lives are excruciatingly short and constantly occur nonchalantly and rather vacuously between life and death.

The towering rollercoaster emotions of desperation and desire are unquestionably the two greatest, most phenomenal forces available in our lives. In certain instances these two emotions are entwined together, after all it's the feeling of desperation that can evoke the push & pull of desire, when the luxury of choice doesn't exist. Of course the emotion of desperation can just result in feeling desperate, lost & destitute. Otherwise, purely by default anyone that goes through the ragged emotions of desperation would rock their world with powerful desire and create a change in their circumstances, successively achieving all they want and need. By that measure surely we wouldn't have homeless, unemployed, helpless or starving people in the world. They would have all conjured magic in their worlds and conquered all the consequences of desperation and loss. In fact we would all welcome a little desperation, if it meant the result was desire, knowing the aftermath of which would give us everything we craved for.

1. Everyone has a 'delicious toffee fudge' that is within their grasp, the tragedy is most people are either unwilling to take the risk, undertake the exceptional effort or suffer the possibility

of associated consequences to actually reach out for it. Yet the prize of actually achieving the metaphorical 'delicious toffee fudge' is awe-inspiringly massive. The significance of such attainment is far greater than reaching the desired acquisition. It's the mental development and advancement associated with reaching the goal that's most commendable and important to further development in life. Every occasion a 'delicious toffee fudge' is acquired, our mental capability to reach out even further than before is exacerbated. Simply, the more you achieve the more you become capable of achieving.

2. An even greater tragedy than not pursuing your personal 'delicious toffee fudge', is not having a desire or need for such a physical or emotional requirement. There are few people in this world that are unconditionally content with all they have. In the multitude of human cases it's the burdensome and reluctant acceptance of their current situation, bound by the fear that they are incapable of reaching out any further than the hand of cards they've been dealt. Ironically fear may stem people into their self-nurtured boundaries, however fighting the fear of failure and actually having a motivating desire is far more colossal in comparison to the ability required to actually achieve it.

One doesn't have to physically and emotionally live through a fifty one minute car crash drama to make life-changing decisions or to even see life with renewed perspective. Our environment fuels our understanding and judgement of life and its vulnerability, particularly its ability to cease at the drop of a hat.

September 11ᵗʰ 2001

Ninety two people boarded American Airlines flight 11 at Boston USA travelling to Los Angeles, whilst sixty four people boarded United Airlines flight 77 for the same journey. On this day these two flights plus a further two flying across America were about to make international history and potentially change the course of the entire world. The date was September 11ᵗʰ 2001.

At approximately 8.25am the horrific realisation that five of the ninety two passengers on board flight 11 from Boston had a very divergent and twisted motive than travelling to Los Angeles, they apathetically hijacked and took control of the plane, the consequences of which shook the world to oblivion. At 8.46am unimaginable tragedy, as the plane was diverted on a journey of unscrupulous misery, and wanton destruction and was ploughed directly into the north tower of the World Trade Centre in New York.

It's difficult even beginning to contemplate or imagine the personal catastrophes caused by the attacks on the infamous September 11th 2001, they were heinous crimes against humanity and no matter what the cause, will forever remain detestable and a disgraceful loss of innocent lives.

This historic catastrophe was a milestone on a global scale directly affecting billions of people one way or another from their beliefs, to their ideology, attitude and thinking. Of the countless thoughts and emotions I've personally endured about September 11th 2001 and its ongoing aftermath, it was the abominable twenty one minutes in the lives of the eighty seven passengers of flight 11 from Boston between 8.25am when the plane was hijacked to hitting the World Trade Centre at 8.46am that are particularly poignant and has created another landscape altering phenomenon during the course of my life. The emotional trauma they suffered is inconceivable from total disbelief and uncontrollable hysteria to panic stricken repenting to God. Twenty one minutes when you're almost convinced your life is now in countdown mode with the reality of death looming seconds away, the sheer remorseless crush in your heart as you see the plane's unwavering decent into Manhattan heading for assured disaster, worse (and we don't know this for sure), if the hijackers had made their hateful intentions clear to the passengers. Between irrepressible prayers begging for salvation and frantic gut-wrenching tears there are heart-breaking pleas to the hijackers but it's pointless, falling on brain-washed deaf ears, their objective is plain and simple, death, mutilation, martyrdom and revenge against America and the Western World. I literally have no conception of the reality those eighty seven passengers and the passengers of the other three planes witnessed but often I've hypothesised about being in that dreadful situation, of only having minutes of contemplation left, the frantic discontented thoughts that would whizz through my tortured mind. How much of my life would I be content with? How much would I have changed? How much have I left unsaid? How much have I regretted saying? And most disturbingly, what would I do if this plane would change course and land safely?

If all the passengers on those fated flights had somehow miraculously survived from the brink of death, each and every one of their lives would have dramatically changed course. The stark realisation of how our futile lives can be indiscriminately washed away, snuffed out like a candle in the wind without a moment's hesitation is an alarming reality very few people comprehend and when they do envision the futility and fragility of life its often too late, as they're about to face their doom and meet the grim reaper. For the fortunate ones that are luckily saved from their predestination of death there is often a renewed understanding, a clarity on life like never before, then imaginatively they look further than the hand they were dealt with and make the changes that were once upon a time fraught with obstacles or changes they'd never even imagined.

CHAPTER 6
Imagination

'Looking beyond what is right in front of you is a right you're blessed with. A superior ability like no other, the beginning of all achievement, of all outcomes, of everything you DESIRE. From that spark of imagination will arise your inspiration, the foundation and cornerstone of your entire future and what you want it to ultimately become.'

The faculty of imagining or of forming mental images, or concepts, of what is not actually present to your senses, imagination is specifically a human gift, granted to us above all other animal life in existence. No other animal has the pleasure and privilege of knowing the many wonders that imagination beholds.

Imagining is the ability of forming mental images, sensations and perceptions, in a moment when they are not perceived through sight, hearing or your other senses. Science and Literature are great examples of what comes directly from our unique ability of imagination. It helps provide meaning to experience and understanding to knowledge, it is a crucial facility through which people make sense of the world and it plays an instrumental role in the learning process.

Accepted as the innate ability and process of inventing complete empires within the mind, the power of imagination allows people to live infinite lives and encounter infinite situations, all in short periods of time with no physical foundation. The advancement of the human species is as a direct result of having this exclusive power. People had to imagine the future, to perceive what they wanted, before they took the evolutionary steps of designing it.

Looking beyond what is right in front of you is a right you're blessed with. A superior ability like no other, the beginning of all achievement, of all outcomes, of everything you DESIRE. From that spark of imagination will arise your inspiration, the foundation and cornerstone of your entire future and what you want it to ultimately become.

Imagination, by nature has the freedom of external limitations and therefore can become a source of absolute pleasure and conversely of unnecessary suffering. Consistent with this idea of mental involvement, imagining pleasurable events is found to engage emotional circuits involved in emotive perception and experience, in other words you actually live the experience without living it.

The Witches

The three scowling, cackling grotesque witches were flying through the deep blue sky. Their tangled grey hair flowing behind them, their dusty rags bellowing around their scrawny bodies. Deep set eyes in their skeletal faces were crimson with rage. I knew they were coming to get me, as I saw them through the misty bathroom window. I was frozen watching the spectacle, unable to manoevere, unable to call for help. My gaze was transfixed, speechless I just stared in fright. This was the most terror-stricken I'd ever felt, even in comparision to the freakish happenings in recent months and those had single-handedly, managed to wipe the floor clean where ghastly, mysterious happenings were concerned. This was it, all my inappropriate, graceless & sacrilegious behaviour had summoned these bloodcurdling wretches, this was my personal judgement day. They were coming to destroy me with intense pain and suffering. Their journey was almost in deliberate slow-motion, so the prolonged wait became a spine-chilling tease to my doom.

At the age of fourteen this was not normal, in fact quite the opposite, it was disproportionately unbalanced. Surely and psychologically speaking this mindset, bordering on personality disorder, was more becoming of a child that had suffered trauma, instability and disturbances brought on by a plethora of negative stimuli and distasteful happenings. This seemed to be the foundation and makings of a troubled adult life to follow. An adult life, which in reflection could point to distressing, mental childhood ordeals and firmly lay the blame on upbringing and dysfunctional parenting.

If there was a definition of perfect parenting, a blissful childhood, a story-book contented upbringing, a young life of abundance in unconditional love, attachment, closeness and materialism then mine was as close as it could be. I wasn't even an only-child, which is another psychologist's favourite when pointing the finger at a debilitated young life, leading to a deteriorated and flawed adulthood. There just wasn't anything so conclusive that could shed indisputable evidence, explaining particular actions and consequences that bordered on being dangerously psychotic.

Imagination is generally a discourse from what is previously known, in this case it was seriously stretching its own boundaries, conjuring horrendous macabre images. Images that were so lifelike, that the pending arrival of the flying creatures, had even tinged the air with a decaying putrid aroma, accompanied by a distinct drop in temperature and a sudden cloudy greyness to the mid-morning sunshine.

Was this an example of a young, tortured mind going through some kind of turmoil, creating vivid imagery, usually associated with the special effects department of the film industry, or was it a bizarre reality, a crossover of demons from a dark world unknown to humankind. Whatever this visual horror was it was lucid, terrifying and beyond normal beliefs.

Everything was beginning to make sense, there was a sleepy haziness and unearthly soft focus in the air, my body was rigid unable to move, which meant I was about to wake, of course, it had suddenly dawned upon me this alarming torment was just a ghoulish nightmare. The sense of relief was colossal. I was urging them to speed up their descent, this was a dream, I was invincible. They were now hovering outside the bathroom window gruesome beyond belief, rancid red veins full of pulsating blood racing through their faces, teeth like gravestones and mouths of endless black, like deep tunnels of pending calamity and destruction. Eyes seething with evil condemnation, screaming a thousand deathly curses, for anyone unfortunate enough to stare into them. This was as unpleasant as a nightmare gets, it was intense terror an unfathomable dread. Nevertheless my smugness was overwhelming, I closed my eyes and disappeared, get ready bed here I come.

Blood-curdling disaster, I didn't materialise in my bed, I was still there with the devils creatures, they were now howling and screeching with delight, as if they had orchestrated my inability to wake from this fiendish hell. Every pore in my body dripped a cold sweat and cried with devastating agony, yet I couldn't scream, my voice was nothing more than a dry caustic croak, every attempt burnt like acid going down my throat.

This was real, this was my hellish reality, this inexplicable and indescribable abyss was all mine. The underworld had risen and come to me. Fire & brimstone had come to a semi-detached house in Coventry.

My body trembled and quivered with an almost epileptic shock. Their stare burnt into my eyes and made them throb with an insurmountable piercing sting. All six of their witching eyes paralysed my limbs and succumbed my senses into defeat. There was a grenade in my head a ticking time-bomb, the countdown to its blast was deafening me from inside, it was going to explode and splatter my young brain all over the bathroom. Each tick of the bomb detonated a million brain-cells, each single brain-cell shrieked with grievous submission as its cries echoed through my lifeless body. It's almost as if each morsel of my being had eyes, eyes that were crying, crying that was signifying acute pain.

Then the fierce shrill that ripped through my skin into my blood and stopped my heart beating, they spoke in unison. They didn't show signs of speaking, they did it straight into my body, each word became me, each word stabbed like a knife-throwers blade that hit the target it was supposed to avoid.

'Mend your ways or we will burn your soul, mend your ways or we will burn your soul.'

The words were power, a limitless force that pushed my torso with lightning bolt pressure into the thin plasterboard wall, with such a malicious fury that it smashed it into smithereens. The creatures wailed even louder and with one last grotesque penetrating stare they disappeared, taking with them the atrocious smell and the sickening murky air. They were gone. Their terror was swiftly replaced by the pummelling on the door. My mother had heard the commotion and had hurried up the stairs and was demanding I let her into the bathroom.

By now my eyes had recalled how to cry, tears were cascading down my face this was not a normal happening for a fourteen year old boy to witness. The scene that presented itself to my Mother would have devastated the most hardened and oblivious parent.

My crying face was a picture of frozen abject terror, a broken wall with me helplessly lying in the rubble, stretching out a feeble arm to be rescued. I can only try and imagine the dreadful heart-breaking emotions my Mother was going through.

I told my bathroom story again and again in intricate detail. My parents blamed my hellish demise on themselves, the demons would never have left their forbidden world had they taught me more about God. In their credulous religious world, beliefs extended to a dark-side, an opposite to good, a world that was death, destruction and eternal suffering. A world possessed by all that is evil and all that is dead in our living world, a dark-side of ceaseless torment, one that only ever materialised when you abandoned the hand of God. They had unwittingly created my infernal, demonised world. They were single-handedly responsible for not warding the evil existence that haunted me. It should have been easy with the virtues and supremacy of God. Instead, they had let me fall into purgatory, a nether world, a bottomless pit of revulsion, horror and fear.

As parents they were crushed and aggrieved, their distress would stay with them until their dying days. This satanic crazed episode was only months after my debilitating self-induced coma. Mum and Dad had failed to keep their side of the bargain they had failed to keep their child safe from harm. They had failed as parents.

Subsequently, following this macabre chapter in my unlived life, there were lengthy absences from school and exceptionally inscrutable thoughts in my head. Thoughts that plagued me, taunted me and most of all continued to disturb those around me that cared. Naturally, such experiences have their toll on behaviour. It wasn't long before my erratic attitude was beginning to be noticed and before I knew it, I was reluctantly sat before a social worker and a psychologist, who upon hearing my tales of witchery and beastly goings on, were hurriedly writing notes and staring at me like I was a two-headed creature from the unknown depths of imagination. In their defence they had probably never heard such an outlandish and horrific drama, particularly from a child. I'm certain at one point whilst regaling them with my bathroom episode, which I naturally embellished, I could see them recoil with total revulsion. That physical reaction and contorting of their faces spurred me on even more. What power ones imagination could behold, even enough to give mature adults the jitters. The session came to, what seemed like an abrupt end. They closed their notepads and went to concur in an adjoining room. They were absent for a few minutes, enough time for me to take a quick peek at one of their note pads. That was on a Monday, by the Wednesday of that very same week, I had been referred to a child psychiatrist. Upon reflection, my referral was no surprise, in those few snatched moments when I took a sneaky look at the notebook, scrawled in big letters, was the damning conclusion *'Nightmares of a TORTURED MIND, needs immediate attention, possible danger to himself and others'.*

My emotions were a peculiar mix of hysteria, disdain, curiosity and most of all gratification.

Wednesday afternoon in a musty smelling, dimly lit room. Huge oak shelves full of large leather bound books with titles that have remained burnt into my memory 'Without hope the heart truly dies', 'Think and Grow Rich', 'Overcoming Mental Abuse', 'The Power of Positive Thinking' I remember those four titles lucidly. I recall myself wondering if such provocatively titled books really had the answers people were searching for and whether the authors of such publications had to suffer any afflictions, downfalls and challenges before they were qualified to write and comment on these subjects.

'Are you interested in these books', was the opening line from Rosemary the psychiatrist, who seemed to appear from nowhere, although in reality I just hadn't noticed she had arrived, as I was engrossed by what I now know as personal-development books.

'No I'm not, I wasn't looking at the books, there are evil eyes staring at me from the book-shelf.'

Rosemary turned to the shelf with a panic-stricken face and removed the four titles and placed them in-front of me, she was clearly shaken, almost as if she had seen the evil eyes staring at her too.

Her voice was warbling *'Are they still staring?'*

'Yes, they are' I shrilled and disturbingly pointed at the gap left by the removed books.

Her complexion changed instantaneously, from a pale, rosy-cheeked face to a blotchy, ruddy colouration. *'Okay describe them to me.'*

With my intonation higher and with a dramatic distressed expression I started, *'They are blood red and angry, they want me dead, they want to kill you too, they are looking at you. They're burning into your head. You are going to die. You're going to hell.'*

Well, that was the end of my first phsychiatry session. My parents, who were waiting outside were called and I suspect, judging by the dejected look on Rosemary's face, she never wanted to see me again and she never did.

I guess by now you've ascertained there were no eyes staring and I got nothing from that session, except a fascination with Personal-Development books. I never saw Rosemary ever again, neither was I ever referred to any other specialist, other than the Soothsayer and fraudulent Exorcist. Now that wasn't due to a miraculous recovery from my 'tortured mind', it was more as a result of not wanting to put my parents through any further anguish. I had already inflicted enough unnecessary injury and pain upon them. It was time to make amends.

Imagination had proved itself to be hugely powerful, not only in changing personal perception and mindset but in actually persuading others to make some obscure judgements and physically affecting their awareness.

The abhorrent bathroom occurrence both proved how a mind can work under stress and how capable imagination really is.

An ordinary morning with the usual sleepy and reluctant sojourn into the bathroom. Nothing spectacular, just an everyday routine that resulted in a grief-stricken social worker, child psychologist and psychiatrist, months of specialist observation, thoughts and happenings so realistic that they still scare the living daylights out of me, traumatised parents, weeks off school, a very first introduction into personal development but most importantly an acute understanding and respect for the power and necessity of imagination.

Let's take a step back, right back to entering the bathroom half asleep. Moments before the grotesque creatures flew into my life. I grabbed the toothbrush, squirted an appropriate amount of toothpaste onto the bristles and without hesitation did what comes naturally, started to vigorously brush my teeth. In fact, I brushed them so vigorously the toothbrush slipped off my teeth straight into my upper gum, with a searing pain it ripped the soft flesh and made it bleed into my mouth and all over my pearly teeth. OUCH!! It really did hurt and agitated me. After much swilling my mouth with water, the bleeding subsided. I recommenced brushing my teeth, rather gingerly this time. Damn, much to my displeasure and annoyance I slipped again and pushed the toothbrush straight into the smarting wound, which subsequently poured out another stream of blood. It was making me angry now but I was determined to finish cleaning my teeth. Blood mixed in with the white paste, morning tiredness and now completely irritated at the result of my clumsy brushing, I rapidly persevered. To my utter disbelief it happened again. The toothbrush careered straight into the already bleeding wound and ripped another slice of gum, with a pain that can only be described as a hot scalpel cutting through a previously healed wound but this time with an even deeper and angrier incision. I was incandescent with rage and in that moment of sheer suffering and momentary madness, I lashed out at the wall with an almighty kick. My frenzied and idiotic attack against the inanimate parting caused an extraordinary chain-reaction. It cracked with a tremendous noise causing a gaping hole, rubble and dust fell to the floor and into the carnage I lost my balance and tumbled. Cue my mother's frenzied knocking at the door.

In that split second following my self-created bedlam, just before I opened the door to my hysterical Mother, my imagination went into massive overdrive. It was driven by the potential consequences of my erratic and anger fuelled behaviour. With that cloud of doom and apprehension, without an ounce of reverence for my Mother and all in the bat of an eye, the epic distortion of the truth began and the chronicle of the beastly witches gave birth.

I didn't have a 'tortured mind', neither was I psychotic. I was nothing more than a LIAR. Deceitful, deceptive with an ingenious and quick-witted imagination, one that was readily utilised to get me out of sticky situations and conceive a flabbergasting, delusional world that bordered on the preposterous and yet managed to convince or unnerve so many people, from personal connections to professional bodies.

Whatever your thoughts on my contemptuous, sacrilegious and generally obscene behaviour, in particular towards my parents, those vivid projections and images in the dark corners of my imagination, took me to a world where the line between fantasy and reality was an extremely thin one.

The witches in the bathroom filled me with consummate dread and fear, even though they were never even there. I repeated and retold the story so many times they became a permanent fixture in my brain, so authentic that I genuinely believed they had really existed. Even now decades on, whilst I'm writing about those disturbing interludes of my life, I'm experiencing a tingling, creepy shiver down my spine. I'm sat in a hotel room and I've just caught myself taking a quick cautionary glance at the window, it's been more than thirty years and yet I still expected to see those flying beasts, they are so still so animated in my mind. C'mon Michael, this is farcical, that whole misadventure was fictitious, an outright figment of your imagination. It never bloody happened. For three decades I've endeavoured to put that particular phase of my life into perspective, however here we are today and it still has an extraordinary effect on my character. No matter how many times or in how many ways I've tried to convince myself of this self-created nonsense, it still strikes a chord of grotesque reality, even to this very moment as I tap the words of this book on my laptop. The aftermath of my self-inflicted parody doesn't stop there, the home where I grew up still exists, as does the bathroom within it. I regularly go back there to visit my family and I still avoid using that bathroom, on the odd occasion I've had no choice to ascend the stairs and take that vivid and ludicrous step back into my shocking history. As you can imagine I loathe using that bathroom and to this day I haven't glanced through the top section of the window, just in case the obvious transpires. The very wall that I demolished during my demonic morning with the slap-dash slip of a tooth brush still carries the scar of my anger. Underneath the wallpaper there is a distinct ridge where the repair was carried out, the very sight of that faint jagged section, unnoticeable to anyone else, causes me untold anguish and heartbreak, that at times has then proceeded to affect my entire day and spirit.

We all possess thousands of memories that are triggered by a whole hoard of stimuli. We have the ability to store, retain and recall information and experiences. Memory is a complex brain-wide process that begins with encoding then proceeds to storage and eventually to retrieval. However, the emotional memories that are recalled by me, through various associated stimuli are not based on any actual physical experience. The events from over thirty years ago, never actually happened, they were entirely fabricated, a total misrepresentation of the truth, as counterfeit as you can get.

Based on my witches and that entire juvenile interlude of my life I can categorically conclude that our imagination is a cornerstone of desire, success and a fruitful future. It can be the difference between mediocrity and eminence. If an innocent trip to a bathroom can trigger such a horrific mixture of memories and emotions from a situation that was only ever perceived and never actually materialistically happened, then one of the greatest inert talents we are blessed with is our wonderful and stunning imaginations.

Our subconscious mind understands feelings and reacts towards them, that subconscious mind can be filled with imagery, creativity, invention and ingenuity of absolutely anything we want.

What if my mischievous mind had created positive affirmations instead of ghastly, intimidating, hair-raising images it did? There is absolutely no doubt that power would have created a very different life for me, it's difficult to imagine where my mindset could have taken me. Instead of witches I could have visualised a life of abundance, of contentment and all the associated emotions that go with that. The witches could have been bearing great advice and riches that would have conditioned me in a very different way. In a way that trips to the family bathroom would now be extremely joyful instead of intimidating and frightening. Nevertheless, what happened had to happen how else would have I got myself out of the tom-foolery I'd created?

Your Bomb

Our lives are governed by an emotive map which is segregated with turning flashpoints and cornerstones, points that determine our behaviour and direct the paths we travel. These landmarks are created through our experiences and our congenital ability to have the power of thinking. This ingrained, astonishing ability acutely separates us from all God's less fortunate beasts that without such an inherent capability will always be dominated by humans, no matter how ferocious, deadly and commanding the animal is, it'll always be lagging behind on the evolutionary scale without the dexterity of deliberating, evaluating, rationalising, speculating and pertinent life-governing cornerstones and therefore will always make us the most powerful creatures that walk this earth. On the contrary our innate and distinguished life qualifications also bequeath us with the capacity to destroy ourselves, obliterate the planet and harm others for no other reason than personal gratification and power, which if the animal kingdom had the mastery to realise, would undoubtedly bestow upon them the superiority status in God's kingdom.

Through curiosity and imagination there are life-changing and perception altering cornerstones available to everyone. When you open your front door what do you see? If it's your front garden, fence and the street you live on (or whatever your frontage looks like), then you have yet to locate your buttons and exercise your curiosity in your dormant mind. If all you can see is what is in your direct vision then at least 90% of your brain is passive, lethargically allowing you a life of mediocrity. What about when you look in the mirror? What do you see? If it's your face and that's all, then that's all you have, your depth is your reflection, which is contradictory to the power you have in that seemingly empty skull you're nonchalantly gazing upon.

Opening your front door is metaphorically opening the door to possibility, possibility which is hindered by the restrictions of your own barricading fencing. There is a time-bomb ticking away in your head, it's timed to detonate at a very precise moment. That monumental, precise moment is the very moment your physical ability to seek out, explore and experience all those things that the dormant 90% of your brain is currently hiding from you will no longer be possible. Sadly your time-bomb explodes moments before you take your last breath of life, its timed to shatter and plague you with the shrapnel of everything you should have, could have done, suddenly for one moment only, your sleeping 90% brain awakens to torture your mind with the possibilities and potential that have now been snatched from you.

The noise from your personal ticking time-bomb should be deafening to the point of distraction, it should keep you awake at night and interfere with the very essence of every action and every thought you have. Open your front door, visually smash through your flimsy fence and soar into the curiosity and haze of the unknown. Let your fixed gaze burn through everything in your path, in your exalted quest to discover life affirming cornerstones.

When you look in the mirror, it's not just a face you see. Look deep into your eyes and visualise your ticking time-bomb, a spherical grenade packed full of soul destroying carnage and shrapnel of belated intangible possibility. There is a question mark on the timer, there is no actual time, it merely reads *'minus one minute from departure'* You have no idea when it will detonate but you do understand detonation only happens when you've reached your expiry date, to be precise one minute before you depart this world, when the contingency and capacity to encounter and encourage your potential have completely evaded your life.

Look closer and you'll see a pull-ring next to the 'minus one minute' timer. That pull-ring if activated immediately detonates your time-bomb and the incessant ticking in your head instantaneously stops. Unfortunately, 90% of your brain is uninspired and dormant and is refusing to awaken until its 'minus one minute from departure', its in a comatose state of inactivity only motivated by your pending termination. Therefore its no surprise why the majority of people are bedraggled and weighed down with the overwhelming regret of everything they could have experienced and achieved.

Imagine if you could detonate your time bomb the next time you look in the mirror, the explosion would manifest and conjure a tumultuous array of possibilities, promise and potential. Your usual reflection would be transformed into a magical array of images picturing the way you want your life to be, packed full of the desire and beauty you had long forgotten or never even considered. In this enchanted scenario the scene as your life reaches 'one minute from departure', would be rewritten into a masterpiece of satisfaction, bliss and comfort, knowing that you left no stone of personal accomplishment unturned, a life fulfilled with a heart full of atonement, pleasure and pride.

This awe-inspiring depiction of a totally bewitched departure is within your grasp. Naturally such a passionate, consummated and sensational life requires an almighty, powerful shift in thinking, ideology, belief, vision and hope but it is possible. A significant, convincing perception of the symbolic time-bomb, relentlessly ticking away in your mind, awaiting your impending doom and the harsh, bitter consequences it beholds is an exquisite starting point. That very concussive explosion 'one minute from departure' is a Pandora's box of regret, when every unsatisfied morsel of your existence is brutally spewed into your mind, creating an exhibition of remorse, guilt, anguish and distress and the overwhelming penitence that you're helpless to make amends. Those merciless parting emotions are the ones that accompany you to your grave. What a melancholy, regretful end to a glorious life that had so much promise, possibility and potential.

'Opening your front door is metaphorically opening the door to possibility, possibility which is hindered by the restrictions of your own barricading fencing. There is a time-bomb ticking away in your head, it's timed to detonate at a very precise moment. That monumental, precise moment is the very moment your physical ability to seek out, explore and experience all those things that the dormant 90% of your brain is currently hiding from you will no longer be possible.'

CHAPTER 7

Regret

'The cumbersome affliction of regret is a considerable anchor to bear, steadfastly mooring you to the situation with the ineptitude of mentally moving on, particularly in some circumstances where it is impossible to indemnify yourself, make amends, or simply just say sorry.'

A long poisonous, spinning, serrated knitting needle-like spike, with a razor sharp tip burning red hot and capable of penetrating any material, its power, sharpness and crippling ability powered by the most virile form of electricity available, the persistent hindrance of negative human thought. This is the destructive sword of regret, which burrows with its glowing burning point into the brain and is capable of causing carnage in every tiny morsel of existence. Relentless, inexorable punishment, a negative conscious and emotional reaction to personal past acts and behaviours, a feeling of sadness, shame, embarrassment, depression, annoyance or guilt, after one acts in a manner and later wishes not to have done so.

Regret can describe not only the dislike and antagonism for an action that has been committed, but also, importantly, the remorseful regret of inaction. Something that should have been said or done that wasn't.

Either way, whether it's regretful action or inaction, in the multitude of situations, the moment has passed and no matter how we try to compensate, apologise or make amends the particular moment that would have made all the difference in the situation and most imperatively in our minds has been lost in time and gone forever.

Carnage

Every single day Monday to Friday the very same journey, accurately following the very same daily actions, in other words, a strict routine, one that strategically facilitated arrival at my work desk at 9.00am every morning. Alarm rings at 6am, reluctantly wake up and crow bar myself out of bed at 6.15am, go to the bathroom, get dressed, have the same breakfast and leave the house at precisely 7.20am, drive through the circuitous side roads and collection of roundabouts and finally at 8.00am, arrive at the motorway junction, a methodical system precisely timed to avoid the rush hour calamities of heavy traffic, so precise that even arrival at the motorway junction two minutes later at 8.02am had its ramifications.

31st August 1999, buzz, buzz, buzz, its 6am on another normal weekday. The alarm buzz signifies another fifteen minutes of warm bed bliss before the day begins. On cue the 6.15am buzzer sounds. On any other day, as has been the habitual routine for over three years, the 6.15am buzz should have meant leaping out of bed and bounding towards the bathroom. Not today, uncharacteristically and for no other reason, than the fact it just felt right to stay in bed for another fifteen minutes, I didn't get out of bed until 6.30am, totally aware and with the understanding the extra fifteen minutes of lethargy had the potential domino effect of making me very late for work. Consequently, I didn't reach the motorway junction until 8.17am, approximately seventeen minutes later than normal. Bizarrely, considering I was late, the unexpected fifteen minutes of laziness hadn't even registered as unusual or contrary until the motorway traffic came to a standstill at 8.25am. Disaster, if only I'd ignored my instinct to anomalously stay in bed, I wouldn't be now stuck in bumper to bumper traffic. Irritated and conscience-stricken about my nonchalance for getting to work on time, I switched the radio on to hear the local traffic news to determine the cause of the annoying traffic jam. Typical but depressingly gloomy, it was a multiple and tragic crash involving a lorry, a coach full of children and fourteen individual cars. That day in August, 1999 I didn't reach work at all, the motorway remained closed for the rest of the day and any cars approaching the incident remained stuck until the Police were able to turn the multitude of vehicles around, I finally got back home at 1pm, having travelled no more than twelve miles. A complete waste of a day, entirely because I was reluctant to get out of bed on time, like I had traditionally done so for years.

There were many casualties on that day. Countless people, including children lost their lives, not to mention many others that sustained bloody and dismembering injuries, a journey for some people that ended in an inconceivable and horrendous manner. It made headline news on television, with dreadfully sombre coverage depicting scenes of carnage, loss and desperation along a route very familiar to myself.

Suddenly an appallingly shocking realisation, one that made time stand still and send a quivering, unnerving jolt through my entire body. The on-the-scene reporter said 'at approximately 8.15am a lorry lost control, the result was devastation and a multiple vehicle pile-up. Tonight there are seven people dead, with many more injured. The Police have yet to establish the cause of the accident. It'll be some time before we know what actually happened, as the driver of the lorry also died in the crash. As you can see from the carnage it's hard to believe how anyone could have survived'.

Dazed, confused, bewildered but overall relieved, I had a shocking revelation, had I approached the motorway at my usual time of 8.00am, accurately at 8.15am I would have reached the precise location where the grim bloodshed happened, I could have been part of the headlines, potentially named as one of the victims, or at least one of the multitudes that were severely and critically injured. The day after, upon rising at my normal time of 6.15am and leaving home at the customary 7.20am, I arrived at the motorway junction at exactly 8.00am, much to my chilling confirmation at exactly 8.15am, the time of the crash, I passed the severely burnt and damaged road and contorted and crushed central barrier.

Whatever eccentric, unknown forces of divine intervention, the universe or nature itself were involved one way or another I was saved from my personal judgement day and subsequent appointment with the impetuous and unforgiving grim reaper. Somehow gut instinct, an internal physical and mental sixth sense and eminent intuition simply persuaded me to stay in bed a trifle longer than usual, it naturally and candidly felt absolutely right to do so.

If I had ignored my inherent divination on the 31st August 1999 and arrogantly followed my accustomed routine, it could have resulted in instant death. If I was one of the luckier casualties, escaping death but suffering ghastly injuries or worse the utter malady and pain of an amputation, I sincerely believe I'd still be burdened to this very day with an almighty regret of not following my predisposed gut reaction and celestial aptitude.

Dad

The 31st of August always heralds a distinct, painful and wretched memory for me and opens up the much debated door of the unknown. I was emancipated from the pain and consequences of injury and probably saved from extinction itself. However my angst and attachment run deeper and more sorrowful than the heady salvation of 1999.

31st of August is also the anniversary of my Father's final day on this earth and represents a concise and superlative definition of regret.

I've learnt to accept the inevitability of death and loss, having faced it many times myself and having lost dear, loved ones to that unfathomable and impertinent darkness of no return. In respect of my father the hardship and grievance of his death has been somewhat overshadowed by the gigantic encumbrance and infinity of remorseful regret.

Multiple health issues and challenges in his early sixties had left my father reasonably helpless and confined to hospital for two weeks, the final straw being a debilitating stroke, leaving one side of his otherwise fairly healthy body heartbreakingly paralysed. The hospital was only a few miles away, I owned a car and although I had a demanding job visiting him in hospital wasn't difficult or bothersome. Nevertheless, it was mid-August, the sun was shining and going to hospital was becoming an obligatory chore rather than a heartfelt responsibility. Had I known that he wouldn't witness the month of September and that there were merely days left before he was going to leave us for good, I would have sat by his side every waking second, saying all those unsaid things that just needed to be said, even if they were as simple as 'Thank you' and 'I love you dad'. However, we didn't know his life was balancing on a tightrope strung between the pain and suffering of diseases on earth and the tranquillity, bliss and infinity of the heaven he believed in. We had no idea he had already walked the tightrope further than halfway, so far that a return to this earthly life was fraught with danger and crippling infirmity, there was no looking back now he had to keep walking forward to his promised land.

A phone call at 7pm on the 30th August from my own brother confirmed dad was gradually giving up all hope of turning around. He was walking further away from his family and earthly life. There was a blissful resignation adorning his face, not one of giving up hope but of a much greater hope than humankind, a hope of finding true deliverance, peace and serenity in the hands of the God he had believed in through all his living years. The same God, that had bestowed upon him this wonderment of life, tested him with illness and pain and now was beckoning him back home.

I was being beckoned to hospital, particularly as dad was having one of his rare moments of consciousness and had mustered enough memory, which had recently and rapidly deteriorated, to remember my name and wonder where I was. I was intensely touched by the sentimental moment but was already dressed and preened to go partying that night. Against a deep burgeoning intuition to visit dad that evening, I decided to go out instead, after all I didn't want to let my friends down, I was already spruced up and I'd planned to visit dad the following afternoon straight after work. My mood was anxious and inexcusably crabby throughout the night, in fact I wasn't pleasant company, so I was pleased to finally get back home and get to bed.

The next day was a run-of-the-mill shift at work. The phone was ringing incessantly and there was an excruciating amount of paperwork to conclude as it was the last day of August, as was the case with every last day of every month.

At 2pm I saw my colleague answer the phone as I was busy on the other side of the room, she looked up to attract my attention. At that very second a huge black cloud of despair materialised, time stood still as a lifelong agonising picture slide show began to torture my mind, images of contentment and childhood happiness, surrounded by loving parents doing everything within their power to keep their children happy, a visual haze of glorious, unrepeatable bygone days. An immense foreboding sensation swept through every anxious cell of my body, I knew this wasn't an average phone call from a supplier or complaining customer, a sixth sense feeling of dread punctured and gouged a bleeding hole deep inside my heart and I instantaneously knew my life was about to change for good.

The incredibly uneven path of our lives is littered with poignant landmark moments of total enchantment and biting grief, those very moments powerfully and without hesitation symbolise a massive shift in our perception of life and the world we live in. By their very nature and the power they impose and exhale upon us, these lifelong moments are very few and far between and are ordinarily created around life, death and survival. The very moment a parent witnesses the birth of their child becomes a ceaseless, life affirming memory which in most cases of parenthood turns their lives inside out, never to be the same again. Returning from the cusp of death, miraculously escaping its evil clutches after staring it in the face, precariously balancing on that tightrope between earth and your doom but gallantly returning home creates a mammoth affirmation that will colour the remainder of your grateful life. Such moments are either heavenly and divine or brewed and orchestrated by the devil himself.

That phone call at 2pm on the 31st August 1988 shook my world and created a tremor that has never stopped vibrating, a moment from the dark abyss that typifies a gargantuan shift in perception and my entire understanding of life itself. It wasn't just the news no one ever wants to hear, the death of a loved one but the unimaginable reams of unsaid words and unexpressed emotions that will from that moment on haunt your days and stay unsaid and unexpressed within your tortured mind.

Blank, emotionless, confused and in utter disbelief I drove at breakneck speed to the very ward of the hospital where I should have been last night but was far too selfish, stupid and conceited to consider. It's amazing how our hectic lives of ringing phones, barking customers and demanding Managers come to an immediate standstill when there is an earth shattering moment occurring, nothing in the Universe matters and everything suddenly gains a heady perspective.

The nurses on Dad's ward directed me to the hospital chapel. Emotions intact and with complete composure I was directed by the chaplain to the door with his softly spoken words *'I'll leave you alone with your father'.*

The dark oak door creaked open as I gingerly stepped inside, my eyes had to adjust to the serenely lit dim room. The back wall was draped from the ceiling to the floor with dusky crimson curtains. On either side of the room was a black ornate floor standing candelabra, each with three thick candles, all were burning, except one on the right that was smoking, suggesting it had only just been extinguished, must have been a draught because the smoke was drifting to the right, as were all the flickers from the remaining five candles.

In the middle of the room between the candlesticks was a table also draped in velvety red, upon the table was a disturbing sight, I'd never seen one other than in photographs and on television, it was a coffin. Arrogant, moody and stern it was dark polished oak with shiny brass handles glistening in the candlelight. There was no lid on this daunting, malevolent and yet distinguished casket for the dead. My footsteps were slow each one seeming to echo in my ears as I impassively walked along the wooden varnished floor towards it, somehow trying to delay the inevitable with my tardy, slow-motion jaunt. My head was a jumble of every emotion and erratic confused thought imaginable. As I got closer, I saw the profile of a man lying in the coffin, a very familiar man, one I'd known my entire life. I was still stood at a distance as an uncontrollable deluge of tears gushed from my eyes, my entire body stiffened unable to proceed any further, I was afraid to get any closer, just in case this familiar man didn't wake to greet me.

You're driving an exceptionally powerful car at a reckless whirlwind speed, straight ahead of you is a solid brick wall, you know you'll make impact, you totally understand the impact will be devastating but somehow you're not going to die, be maimed or suffer any crippling injuries. You're magically going to live through this, with one principal, overbearing exception. You will suffer the mental anguish, everlasting sickness, pain and turmoil of the colossal deadly and indescribable encounter. The jeopardy ahead is irrevocably perilous but you have no option to continue this premeditated meteoric, doomed encounter.

Reluctantly I moved forward and grasped the edge of the silk lined, intimidating coffin, an evanescent wave of agitated elation swept over me, a rush of very short-lived excitement. He was just asleep, it was an almighty blunder to put him in a coffin, he didn't look dead, this was Dad's usual state of slumber, one I was accustomed to seeing for decades as he used to fall asleep on the sofa in the living room. Jubilation, all I had to do was wake him up and then I could immediately apologise for my miserly, self-centred behaviour from last night when I should have been at his bedside.

I softly touched his drowsy, sleeping face, synchronised with the humble words 'c'mon Dad, wake up'.

BANG! CRUNCH! Carnage, total devastation, my car hit the wall it was speeding towards and my entire life came crashing and tumbling down, crushed and mashed into an immeasurable seething pile of worthlessness and intense heartfelt suffering.

It was the sudden and shocking realisation that this was death itself. I will never forget that defining moment when my fingertips touched Dad's face, it was pallid, bloodless and sickeningly stone-cold. These closed eyes were never going to open and see life again, this reptilian dead flesh was never going to be warm again, the mouth that lovingly broadcast words of guiding wisdom that always fell on deaf ears, was never going to utter another word, these ears that listened and understood intently, now couldn't hear my mourning, screaming pleas to wake up, my incoherent shouts of repentance of all those unsaid things. It was all gone. This insipid corpse was all that remained, drained and void of life, all those years as a child, adult and father wiped out forever, incapable of even registering the slightest of touch as I held his stony cold, unsympathetic hand and sobbed hysterically.

Until this very day I don't have a solution, procedure or conception of how to overcome, tackle and deal with the burdensome regret surrounding my father's death. Acceptance of my narcissistic, selfish and pitiful behaviour of partying instead of being faithful and conscientious the day before he died has become a way of life. The sentences, words and actions that should have been said at the appropriate moment have become mental establishments that periodically torture and tease my mind. There is no escape from the lurid and equitable punishment of regret.

1. Intuition is the inner perceptive ability to acquire knowledge without interference or the obvious use of reason. In fact there is no rhyme or reason to some intuitive thoughts and emotions. The word itself comes from the Latin word 'intuer' which roughly translated means 'to look inside' or 'to contemplate'. Intuition provides us with beliefs that we cannot necessarily justify. Intuition may well be no more than a combination of mentally stored historical data, deep and heightened observation and an acute ability to cut through the thickness of surface reality. A slow motion mechanism that captures data instantaneously and hits you like a sledgehammer. Intuition could be a knowing and spiritual sensing that is way beyond the conscious understanding, simply a gut feeling. A truly valid perception via the unconscious mind. Whether it is magically mystical or just a mental response to unconscious signals and apprehensions of prior learning, it has an undeniable and powerful inclination. Listen intently to your heart and the ensuing gut-reaction it creates, if something doesn't physically, mentally and emotionally feel right and in some cases even fills you with dread, then don't do it, conversely if the thought of doing a particular action or behaviour fills you with a positive, affirming, warming optimistic sensation, then undoubtedly it's the right thing to do. Maybe it's unreasonable and unacceptable to operate and contrive your entire life utilising this almost intangible methodology but at least negotiate and manipulate your actions when your intuition is unparalleled and the sensation of opposing it is causing apprehension, confusion or zealous doubt. I've had numerous cases of intuitive perceptions during the course of my life, if I had ignored one in particular on the 31st August 1999, there's an immense likelihood I wouldn't be alive today to tell the tale.

2. The cumbersome affliction of regret is a considerable anchor to bear, steadfastly mooring you to the situation with the ineptitude of mentally moving on, particularly in some circumstances where it is impossible to indemnify yourself, make amends, or simply just say sorry.

   a. Destructible Regret – You can make amends and you can positively change the way you feel, not forgetting how you can emphatically influence others, especially if it is the involvement of people that are central to your regretful albatross's. Play the scenario in your mind, imagine rectifying whatever it is causing the regretful sentiment, an apology, an action, whatever it is mull the scene, no matter how cringe-worthy, through your mind, taking into account the conceivable reaction of the person or people concerned. Whilst you're replaying the drama through your thoughts what is your intuitive awareness telling you? A poignant, distinct gut reaction, if you've enacted an acutely honest dramatisation within your mind, will assist you with a conclusion to face and conquer your regrets. If your personal millstone and psychological hindrance is the regret of inaction, then it will stay an encumbrance until you address it with the appropriate action. If the necessary action is within your realms of possibility, then that leap of determination to redress your mental inertia is an invaluable step, go ahead and destroy, crush it, annihilate it, obliterate it from your consciousness. Count your lucky stars you possess that almighty luxury and ability to clean your dishevelled slate of regretful misgivings because there are times when there is no choice for recompense.

   b. Indelible Regret – Painfully inscribed within your heart and etched into your tortured mind are the words or actions that you are now incapacitated from delivering. The person or people involved are dead, or the circumstance is totally irretrievable as the contrary moment has dissolved in history and resurrecting it is an impossibility and totally futile. This is one circumstantial torment I can wholeheartedly relate to, I should have been there. I should have adopted the direction of my hounding, precipitous intuition. The consequential guilt, anguish, shame and secluded bitterness has over the ears left an ingrained and unforgettable scar. Nevertheless, the experience has indoctrinated a stern philosophy and influenced significant decisions during the course of my life, including the overt power and capacity of following my impressionable intuition, which ludicrously in some cases is the very reason I'm still alive today. The reluctant learning process of regret and remorse has been a red hot directional poker, directing my journey in the sometimes confusing, misguidance of an existence that we all have the potential to severely derange. Often we only learn the appropriate navigation of life once we have made the contrite and contradictory mistakes that then command it. Considering the nature of our learning process it is prudent we make our guiding blunders and misconceptions earlier in life, however the true course of life is a comprehensive, incalculable learning process that lasts its entirety and generally we cannot exercise control over the imminent adversities and impending milestones that govern, affect and change our days forever.

'It's over, he's been given less than two weeks to live' was the overwrought, distracted and emotional greeting when I answered the phone to a close friend in October 2010. His father had been progressively unwell and had spent a turbulent few weeks in hospital, concluding with the damning, earth-shattering diagnosis of aggressive cancer. He had been cruelly given the kiss of death that is dreaded by the majority of the world, the inescapable curse and desperation of a disease that has few known everlasting cures, little known inoculation but the dreaded opening of a world embellished with relentless agony, prolonged suffering and torturous anguish. In numerous cases cancer represents an authentic and substantial threat

of death with the potential of broadening sickness and discomfort, even the very mention of the word itself injects a sense of misery into people, stirring awkward and unpleasant memories, as most people know someone who has suffered the scourge of cancer, either as a direct or indirect affliction. Instantaneously my heart plummeted to my boots as sorrowful thoughts of my own father and how much I miss his tender, loving presence flooded my mind with melancholy pictures, accompanied with that age old overwhelming shudder of conscience-stricken regret. Holding back my own selfish tears I hastily recaptured the moment and asked my friend to repeat the controversial statement he had just made, with a sense of emotional fragility in his voice he blurted out the line *'It's over, he's been given less than two weeks to live, its Dad he's going to die'* and without a moment of hesitation I replied *'I'm so sorry. You've got no time to waste otherwise you'll carry the burden of regret around your neck for the rest of your days'.*

Sadly almost two weeks after that conversation his father passed away, the spread of cancer was violent and ruthlessly unforgiving. Losing a parent is a hardship like no other loss, a life bruising strain, a burgeoning pitiless ache, genetically, physically and psychologically irreplaceable, parents are a unique and unaccountable loss to our lives, irrespective of the depth, sentiment or attachment of the relationship we have with them. My friend suffered every human disposition imaginable from anger and resentment to immense sadness and isolated depression, however there was still a beam of shining light surrounding the tremendous bleakness that had tragically fallen upon his life, there was a dazzling spark of solace that lifted him and helped carry him through his dark days, one that will in time to come shine even brighter and positively guide and encourage his personal attributes.

Following the announcement my friend made during that bombshell conversation in October 2010 my advice was quite simple, effortless and crystal-clear. It had been gleaned from decades of regret, from emotions that had been painfully seared into my brain, woven into the very essence of everyday life. I was tactless and abrupt in my approach, I desperately wanted him to accept and understand the vast magnitude of this unfathomable predicament, there was literally no time to be deluded about the outcome or detached from the reality and interpretation of death.

'I really want you to listen and I want you to take action because I don't want you to suffer the sad regret that I have been saddled with since the very day my Dad died, a regret that still weighs me down to this very day. You need to go to hospital tonight and I mean tonight, you need to sit at your Father's bedside and talk to him even though he is unconsciousness he will hear every word. Talk to him about your childhood memories, the laughter the happy days you both shared, remind him of your earliest recollections of life, even tell him a mischievous secret that you've never told him before. Tell him he needs to shake this silly affliction he's got and come back home because his favourite chair is so empty without him and that home just doesn't seem like home anymore. Just hold his hand and talk non-stop and say everything you've always wanted to say, because in two weeks when he is dead it'll be too late and then it'll hit you like a juggernaut when you realise he is no more and will never hear another word from you no matter how loud you shout it out, I know because I remember shouting at my poor Dad, whilst he lay stone cold in the chapel. Do it tonight and then visit him every single last day he has alive but above all tell him how much you love him. Don't miss this chance, one day you will thank me for being so blunt.'

With those tearful and difficultly expressed words resounding in his ears, he did exactly that and went to his father's bedside that very evening and began the heartfelt epilogue which continued until his penultimate days. As the final day approached and his father was gradually giving up hope and rapidly losing the battle against the ferocity of cancer that was weaving death through all his vital organs, my last piece of advice was a final heartrending goodbye.

'Tell him it's time to leave and to not be afraid, there's a beautiful pain-free place waiting for him and that one day you'll meet again. Thank him for being the best father imaginable and that you will look after Mum, then simply hold his hand and tell him you will never forget him and you'll always love him.'

As the coffin started its slow procession along the conveyer belt rollers, into the harrowing fierce, bellowing flames of the crematorium furnace, I knew I'd done my best to guide a friend through his traumatic days and the painful heartbreak he suffered watching his dad die. In years to come as the happier memories start to drown the sadness and loss of a departed loved one, I knew my friend would stand tall with pride and satisfaction that he had said all he needed to say, expressed all his emotions and that his redeeming, joyful and sincere words were the ones ringing in his Father's deteriorating body as he waved goodbye to the world. I also fully understood my advice was borne from my own mistakes, anguish, torturous regret and compassion. If only someone had guided me in the very same way but then again on the contrary would I have had the knowledge, sensitivity and consideration to guide my friend and countless others through the same disagreeable situation had I not suffered the indignity and despair of indelible regret, myself.

One way or another we all suffer the stinging and deplorable agony of regret, sometimes through thinking and acting too fast whilst under the potent influence of anger, fear or desperation, sometimes through not thinking at all, particularly of the potential ramifications of our actions, words or inactions. However, if life was to be so contrived that each action, process and word we spoke was predetermined and acted with forethought and calculation, would our world be terribly predictable and clinically anesthetised? Would we live in a state of indifference and soporific narcosis? Surely, it's the unpredictability of our thought process that creates such wonders of variety and a delicious, colourful potpourri of adventures. It's our unique ability of free will that composes such a mishmash medley world of magic, wonder and surprise, the negative consequences of which can be vast and dangerous from absurd, inhumane wrongdoings to personal blunders resulting in the encumbrance and grief of regret.

Making a mental decision not to do anything regretful in the first place is bordering on spurious and deluded and probably a self-taught arrogance that simply ignores remorseful sensitivities, presumably after encountering and creating numerous regretful situations.

I, myself have learnt to live with my personal cumbersome millstone and find myself regaling people with my story, deeds and inactions, spreading the word to almost anyone that finds themselves in a similar unfortunate situation. It also taught me an invaluable lesson in cherishing people, time and the very existence and vulnerability of life itself because all three are hugely limited and can be wasted or terminated without another breath.

Instinctive, non-meditated reactions, perceptions and awareness has become my powerful weapon against the pestilence of regret, we all have that anonymous sixth-sense, an inherent ability that gives us a sense of foreknowledge, almost a second sight and intuition between right and wrong, between what we should or shouldn't say or do. Wherever that extrasensory perception comes from let it nourish your mind and exercise its awe-inspiring competence through your gut-reactions and constitutional instincts.

There will be regrets and remorseful milestones, you cannot avoid that, it's our inherent and provocative nature and the way we, as human beings learn and develop, it's absolutely fundamental to our mental growth. We are all apprentices of life, so accept the burdens you carry but lighten the load and compensate for the damage by using it as a valuable educational device to guide and steer the remaining days of your life and possibly the lives of others.

CHAPTER 8

Death

'Everyday thousands upon thousands of people feel their ticking time-bomb mercilessly explode revealing all the possibilities they had but didn't take. Everyday people lose someone to the unknown and then predictably wish they'd done or said something differently.'

The end of life, the permanent cessation of all biological functions that sustain a living organism, brought on by old age, diseases, accidents, trauma resulting in terminal injury, suicide, murder and in many parts of our world, malnutrition. For millions of years the nature of death has been a concern to human societies. Religions have various explanations surrounding the consequences of death from resurrection to reincarnation, whereas certain cultures and schools of thought such as atheism don't believe in either, for them consciousness permanently ceases to exist and a state of oblivion, mental blackness, complete inadvertence to living is reached, to them the end really is the end.

Religions either celebrate death as a freedom from the living hell known as earth, paving a way to the celebrated and blissful fields of ambrosia and fluffy white clouds in God's own home known as heaven or the reawakening as another living organism, decided by their goodness, morality and behaviour in their current life, of which living the most devout, god-fearing and virtuous life without sin will return you to earth as a prosperous, healthy human, or on the contrary a sacrilegious and wicked existence will hand you a return ticket to the life of a downtrodden miniscule creature. In alternative societies and comprehensions death just represents nothingness a black void of unconscious darkness, a place of timeless non-existence.

Whether it's a route to the enchantment and paradise of heaven, the bottomless pit and pandemonium of fiery hell, the return to earth in the embodiment of another of God's own creations or an absolute void and total annihilation of life, one stern fact is a consummate certainty, there are people left alive that will never see you on this earth again.

The aftermath and conclusion of death is sporadic, uncommitted and ambiguous, this is not casting aspersions on the beliefs of billions of people who have a definitive faith that their earthly demise leads to enlightenment, awakening or reincarnation, it's my humble opinion based on the absence and deprivation of any substantial proof. Everything our world acknowledges, understands and believes about death is hypothetical speculation whether the views are atheistic and disbelieving or religious and God-fearing. The one thing that is factual, calculated and confirmed is our mortality, that our life is ruthlessly limited and our departure wholly unpredictable. The ethos of our breathing, spirited earthly limitations brings about two poignant questions.

1. Do we truly understand how restricted the extent of our life really is?

2. Do we truly understand the people that we have in our lives have the same unstable and fickle time on earth?

Naturally, one cannot spend every waking, living moment in a traumatised state of mind oppressed with the brutal fear of dying or the death of loved ones, that would lead to a most erratic and abnormal existence. However, merely affirming and recognising the selfish shortness of life may encourage a difference in our outlook, acknowledgement, enthusiasm and philosophy and possibly advocate the lives we dream of, rather than the ones we have saddled ourselves with through the consequential path of just living and humbly accepting.

'I understand how you feel' were the words of condolence I idiotically and unknowingly offered to a dear friend bereaving the untimely death of her father. In her emotionally stirred and agitated temperament she scowled an angry statement at me which has stayed with me forever and disturbingly hit home when I suffered my first loss, the day my own father died.

'You don't know how I feel, how dare you say that. I feel like my world has ended, I feel like my sun won't rise tomorrow. Yours will, your day will be bright, I don't even want the sun to rise. One day you will lose your dad then come back and tell me you know how I feel.'

At the time I put her unreasonable angst down to the emotional turmoil she was suffering. However she was absolutely right I had no conception of what she was going through and how the pain of loss was burrowing into her heart and tearing her life to shreds. Almost a decade after her father had passed away I did contact her, as she had suggested and I apologetically told her I now completely understood how she felt. She cried on the phone, we cried together, we now had a mutual judgement on the meaning of all consuming pain.

The extraordinary concept of permanently losing someone heartfelt and emotionally connected is unfathomable. The very consideration that you cannot physically see, touch or hear that person ever again, let alone speak to them and feel their warmth is wildly eccentric and melancholy to say the least.

My personal interpretation of the two questions above only materialised following the death of my father, sometimes one has to witness an earthquake to understand the effect and magnitude of an earthquake. I had to witness death and bereavement to ascertain its meaning and affect on life and the very essence and confinement of our time alive on this planet. The repercussions in my life were vast and incessant, the sun still rose but I counted every sunrise as a countdown to my final one, each day it dawned upon me, this sunrise could be the penultimate one or even the crowning last masterpiece to shine its light upon me. I began to live my life in a hedonistic, haphazard, irrepressible rollercoaster way, more curious and furious than ever before, now fuelled with even greater impatience and anger constantly aggressing and provoking my regret filled tortured mind. There was no time for balance, moderation or control, life was now just too short to settle for second best and subserviently bow down to the antagonism, negativities and contrary attitudes of people and mediocre living. Every miniscule aspect of my life changed from my relationships, my career, overriding philosophies on life to my enduring belief that everyone around me will, without any or very little warning, disappear to God's heaven, Satan's purgatory, a cadaverous black-hole of oblivion or return as one of God's multitude of creatures.

Our creation is uniquely miraculous, whether it was the religious sanctity of God, or the absolute marvel of science, it is still an omnipotent, phenomenon that we exist and that we exist as human beings that have the supreme, powerful gift of free will and imagination. With so much vision, hope and possibility shining a contradicting pathway away from mediocrity, in an insufficient and awkwardly cramped life that will always end catastrophically, why wait until the death of a loved one before having your own epiphany and rebirth?

The entire Universe is heavily laden with people wishing they had seen the shimmering beacon of light, the one that now represses their soul, casting a bleak shadow over it because they've reached the end of the road or that callous, irreverent roadblock has been reached by someone they loved, cherished and adored. Everyday thousands upon thousands of people feel their ticking time-bomb mercilessly explode revealing all the possibilities they had but didn't take. Everyday people lose someone to the unknown and then predictably wish they'd done or said something differently.

Every single living person, all of us, we're all doomed to face that murky abyss that patiently awaits us. There is no guarantee of nirvana, there is no promise of returning as a reincarnated human being, the only solid, legitimate assurance we possess is one way or another, whether in a ruthless crematorium furnace or six foot under the apathetic, cold ground, we will be nothing more glorious than ashes or dust. We will either nourish the ground we ungratefully walked and lived upon or with a puff of smoke, casually pollute the sky we should have visualised our vast possibilities in.

Embroiled in the indisputable quandary that our demise is unconditional and totally incalculable, it is paramount to understand the gargantuan importance and validity of the two questions. It is vital to convert the questions into authoritative statement answers, with the associated visual images that will form the foundation of your future thinking, actions, relationships and achievements.

1. My life is limited.

2. The people in my life, that I cherish also have limited lives.

November 2010, I arrived early for the funeral of my friend's father. It's a cheerless, dreary day. I'm impatient, downhearted and nervous, for no reason in particular than the sadness of the occasion and an unyielding, forlorn reminder of my personal losses and how much I miss having those dear, beloved people in my life. Funerals have a tendency, beyond the melancholy darkness of the day, to stir a menagerie of menacing and anxious emotions, from mourning the dead person whose funeral you're attending, reflections of past forfeits and indelible regrets to disturbing contemplation of your own funeral. The latter sentiment was grossly exacerbated, upon entering the chapel through the wrong door and strutting directly into another funeral. It wasn't so much my foolhardy oversight, for which I profusely apologised to the usher stood within the door way, it was the bothersome sight within the room that agitated me. There were only two mourners.

Naturally, there can be certain circumstances resulting in such a lowly, depressing number of people at someone's last farewell and celebration of life. They may have been heartbreakingly lonely, with very few people in their life or the knowledge of their death may not be widespread enough, hence people may not be aware they've actually died. Withstanding the practical reasons and justifications for only two mourners, it was an exceptionally untoward and dispiriting sight and a mammoth contrast to the hundreds of mourners that turned up to pay their final respects and bid a tearful goodbye to my friend's father. The funeral was a heart rendering testimony to the heroic, greatness that his father had demonstrated during his life, through his countless deeds, wonderful character and genuine compassion, it wasn't a surprise hundreds of mourners from across the country were present, he had touched the lives of many, that would now miss his earthly presence but would fondly remember his sincere kindness and the eternal impression he had left in their hearts.

I may have been unnecessarily judgemental at the sad sight of only two mourners but what desperate existence must one live that only two people are there to remember you. One of the very few heart warming and uplifting things during the dark and disturbing days surrounding the death of my father were the hundreds of mourners, many that had drifted from his life decades ago, that came to his funeral. My father, very much like my friend's father was hugely respected and admired, so much so, that even people that had outstanding bitter grievances and disagreements with him and consequently hadn't spoke to him for years, were present.

One day all of us will be lying in a coffin awaiting burial or cremation, will the number of mourners at our funeral be tantamount to the life we lived, to the hearts we captured, to the loyalty and trust we established, to the friends we supported in their time of need, to the family we cherished and to the love we shared. Will the mourners be dejected with heavy hearts for a true friend lost, knowing that life will never be the same again or will their emotions be coldly dispassionate and unaffected by your demise.

Surely, the attendance at one's funeral, forgiving anomalous contingencies and the obligation of family, is a testimonial biography and verification of fulfilment within the hearts and minds of people. The culmination of your entire life summed up by the abundance of mourners or their dereliction of your farewell and the life you lived. This simple paradigm of life may not incite a massive shift in perception but further aids the perspective and futility of our short existence on earth.

'Naturally, one cannot spend every waking, living moment in a traumatised state of mind oppressed with the brutal fear of dying or the death of loved ones, that would lead to a most erratic and abnormal existence. However, merely affirming and recognising the selfish shortness of life may encourage a difference in our outlook, acknowledgement, enthusiasm and philosophy and possibly advocate the lives we dream of, rather than the ones we have saddled ourselves with through the consequential path of just living and humbly accepting.'

CHAPTER 9

Fight

'Deep within all of us there is a fight, so powerful so strong, it can overcome any fear, any obstacle, any challenge. It can even intimidate and stave off death itself, even when death is at your doorstep staring you in the face, if your reason for living is big enough.'

In every unfortunate extremity that life can dare to throw at you, there is an inner fight that will bludgeon, scrap and force its way through. Deep inside your head is the 'fight' and when your circumstances are plotting against your purpose, dreams or the very continuation of what you consider your idealistic essence and backbone to be, when your habitual subsistence is provoked it will give you the commanding jolt you need. A distinguishing shove of mental reassurance and firmness, the physical brawn you desperately require or the sheer clarity and prominence in your thinking. These heady dormant attributes are triggered in moments of threat and adversity. The misfortune of hysterical blindness and the calamity of a hazardous entrapment in a car that is on its roof, represent just two possible misadventures already featured in this book. In both predicaments my 'fight' was prompted and prodded into action and the resulting idiosyncratic agility encouraged a positive determination and desired result.

There are people that operate their entire lives in the heightened 'fight' attitude, energetically punching, kicking and slamming their way through every single day. Such an amplified disposition has the potential for outstanding and hugely impressive mental and physical achievements of power and endurance. Winners, champions and incomparable protagonists of success use their 'fight' to accomplish their goals, an electrifying trigger that gets them off the starting block every waking day and enthusiastically firing on all possible cylinders.

Stalwarts and audacious purveyors of immense personal accomplishment still have that hidden, reticent 'fight' that pushes and stimulates them in those moments of arduous distress. Their everyday 'fight', essential for winning is an acronym we'll discuss later but simply is:

F   Fear

I   Inspiration

G   Goals

H   Habit

T   Tenacity

Mum

Another night, another hedonist temptation and invite to party with people that make me smile and thoroughly enjoy life. This event was highly anticipated and billed as the event of the spring, bang in the middle of the Easter holidays. It had the potential of becoming a historically, memorable evening. All the essential ingredients of amusing people, romance, music and of course copious amounts of alcohol were going to be involved, not to mention the event was located within a vibrant, stylish and effervescent location in London. An hour into the ninety minute journey and I receive an ominous call from my sister-in-law, ominous because calls from her were rare and usually signalled a problematic situation. As feared it was something negative, my Mother had been rushed into hospital. Every year I could recall from the early days of childhood I'd known Mum to have health challenges. I'd almost become immune to hearing she was back in hospital, this was becoming a regular occurrence.

Until the day my father had died, Mother had been considered astute and ruthless when it came to business matters and equally as ruthless within family circles. Never one to miss a single penny when it came to money or a single argument when it came to her matriarchal presence and authority within the family, a wonderful, kind hearted and generous woman adored by many and feared by many more. Mum was clearly the dominant parent, often leading to the perception that Dad who was naturally passive and timid, was henpecked. Nevertheless, behind every successful, domineering, tenacious person is a dependable, supportive and loyal person, not always the strongest of characters but always there. The connection of the two opposing personalities and attributes creates a perfect symbiotic relationship. That was my parents, a perfect match with each other's weaknesses substantiated by the other's strengths. It was no wonder then that Mother's physical durability and mental keenness rapidly and disproportionately deteriorated without the presence of father's placid and unassuming support, as did her general health.

The scenario, years later, was still very daunting familiar territory. Stirring and emotionally irrational my haunting, regretful memories returned. I'm ready to party and I have an ailing, infirm parent confined to hospital, there was just no escaping the monumental mistake I had made with my father. Even though it was too late to visit hospital, as it was past the official visiting hours, without hesitation I turned the car around and charged back down the motorway to my Mother's bedside. Her condition wasn't serious but the best medicine for both of us was her smile because I'd unexpectedly turned up, albeit looking and smelling like I was about to party.

For six anxious months Mum was in and out of hospital, with every visit unfortunately lengthier than the previous one.

There was no substantial diagnosis of her condition, as it was blamed on a number of ailments. The hospitalisations became so regular that they were no longer a barometer for illness, we were all getting accustomed and invulnerable to the norm of knowing Mum was feeling unwell.

May 2009, another phone call from my sister-in-law and the same, unsurprising news, Mum was back in hospital. This was probably the tenth occasion of the year and although we were getting immune to the fact, it always sent a melancholy shock through the system knowing Mum was still in agony from one sickness or another. This particular gloomy episode and journey back to Mum's second home, the hospital was due to incessant vomiting and the inability to keep any food or drink in her stomach. For weeks and weeks Mum was wired to drips and syringes of saline solution and vitamins that artificially nourished her body, as her incapability to digest food persisted. Albeit, tube feeding was adequate sustenance, it wasn't healthy in the long-term and certainly not a solution. There were a deluge of examinations, analysis, investigative surgeries, done by a multitude of doctors and nurses but still no conclusive answers, still the mystery illness, the failure to digest food continued. Gradually Mum's appearance, health and hope of recovery disintegrated and it seemed that hospital was her permanent residence, no food or drink had entered her mouth for nearly three months now.

On the morning of 20th July, another normal update phone call from my sister-in-law, understandably so, her voice and temperament were more emotional and erratic than usual, woefully Mum's condition had worsened into a state of unconsciousness, partly brought on by the intense pain-killers that had been administered to her to help stave the extreme pain she was suffering. I and a number of Mum's close family went to hospital that afternoon, particularly as a meeting had been arranged by the Doctor assigned to my Mother and our presence had been dutifully requested. There seemed to be an air of consummate dejection in the air, despite the heart warming presence of all Mum's children and her younger sister. We waited with baited breath for the clock to slowly tick to 4pm, the scheduled time of the meeting.

It was time and we were ushered into another room, we were all crestfallen and despondent, there wasn't any possibility this was going to be blessed and jolly news, purely through the ambiguous context of the almost clandestine gathering and the morose expression on the doctor's face.

'Thank you for being here, I'm afraid...' at that very moment upon hearing the doomed words of 'I'm afraid', my heart sunk to my boots, my mind was tortured into mournful submission and tears welled in my eyes. 'I'm afraid' is simply the worse cursed beginning of any sentence delivered by someone in the medical profession. She continued, *'there's no easy way of saying this but your Mother has been diagnosed with pancreatic cancer and we have no idea how long her body can sustain life, it could be days or it could be months, I'm sorry'.*

We were expecting the worse but the very mention of the 'C' word stunned the room into total bewildered and miserable disbelief, even the doctor herself appeared to be depressed and they deal with terminal illnesses on a daily basis, however delivering depressing, sad news is probably as mentally debilitating as the people it directly affects.

An acerbic black cloud had now positioned itself over all of us, steadfastly hovering and drenching us with a downpour of joyless rain. No one was capable of saying much as the tragic reality of becoming orphans was getting closer. Mum was still unconscious so there wasn't anything else that could be done, the advice offered by the nurses was to go home and return tomorrow. I was the last one to make a move to the exit but there was a challenge, every living cell in my body was reluctant to leave, my intuitive gut-reaction was to stay longer and if life had taught me one particularly overbearing lesson, it was to acknowledge my skilful intuition.

Life is governed and created through a set of decisions that one has to make, in fact every decision made, every corner turned, every path travelled has brought you to your current circumstances and mindset. There are times when we have little choice in the decisions we're forced to make, those obligatory compromises are also concocted through the precedence we've set in the past and the previous action we've taken. Nevertheless, it's the life affirming, life altering decisions, the voluntary ones that can dramatically metamorphose our existence and our thinking. Voluntary, autonomous choice is one of the most integral and constitutional abilities we posses, our extraordinary and inherent ability to adjudicate one course of action over another or over a variety of possibilities, utilising our knowledge and experience.

When such a powerful congenital ability is propelled by an internal, almost clairvoyant emotional force, then as we've already learnt with situations notated in this book the choices and decisions we make can herald the difference between life or death and regret or satisfaction.

I suspect the intuitive decision I made to sit by my Mothers bedside for the entire night, will remain one of the most immaculate and sentimentally gratifying decisions I've ever made. That was the last night mum was alive. Intuition had saved me from an ill fated choice that would have burdened me with another colossal regret.

All night Mum was in intense pain, delving in and out of consciousness, with the nurses increasing her dosage of morphine painkillers almost every single hour. Reminiscing about that night will always be hopelessly sad for me and yet ironically it's a night full of beautiful, lasting memories. We spoke about the wonderful person Dad was and about how much he was missed and about many happy childhood happenings, not to mention the shenanigans I was forever embroiled in. In her usual persuasive manner Mum even made me make promises of living a more settled and controlled life and through the pain she was suffering, my usual sarcastic responses forced her to smile and laugh a little. I gently stroked her head while we spoke, in the vain hope it may alleviate some of her heart-wrenching discomfort that was hurting her to the core.

All through the night I was contemplating the despair of a life without parents and the almighty shock of finally discovering Mum's condition and ailing health was caused by the curse of cancer and still, even through the profound melancholy haze, a glimmer of hope, albeit a miniscule flicker, still shone in the distance. There was still hope that Mum could survive this dreaded disease and come back to living her real life again, in her role as the incredibly supportive and characteristically divine woman she was, totally dependable and forever comforting. Unfortunately, normality was never going to be restored, in fact life was about to take another precarious diversion.

Within less than twenty four hours since the diagnosis of cancer, Mum's health had deteriorated rapidly and had reached an irreparably critical stage. At 10am on the 21st of July 2009, in a brief moment of consciousness Mum whispered she could no longer stay alive, she could no longer fight the intense pain and that her last wish was to see her direct family for one final goodbye. Individually, they were all contacted but it was looking very unlikely her dying wish would be fulfilled as some of them were literally hours away. The pain was relentless, so the regular injections of painkiller were replaced with a morphine drip, continuously pumping the powerful sedative into her blood, to ensure her last moments alive were painless and humane as possible. With such a severe dosage of morphine there was less than ninety minutes of life remaining within this tired, fragile and decrepit body, the drug itself becomes responsible for a permanent, peaceful sleep. All the family were rushing to hospital to say their last, sad goodbye and help satisfy Mum's dying wish. At precisely 11.30am and as predicted, at exactly ninety minutes after the morphine drip had been introduced into her arm, Mum started to slowly close her eyes and enter a permanently unconscious state. Miraculously she hadn't passed away yet, sat right next to her I could see and hear the movements of her shallow breathing, the nurses were in disbelief, the pain and dosage of sedative were unbearable but somehow Mum was managing to stay alive. At 12.42pm Mum's last family member arrived and I whispered in her ear and told her, she acknowledged with the faintest facial movement imaginable. At 12.43 one minute after all the family had arrived and had said their tearful farewell, Mum took her very last breath and died. For over one hour Mum had managed to stay alive against all the odds of a body and mind in total shutdown, there was absolutely no reasoning whatsoever, other than to feel and witness the presence of her family before she eventually gave up her will to live and surrender to death. The Doctor that was in charge said Mum had fought with every imaginable ounce of willpower, it was unlike anything the Doctor had witnessed before, to stay alive, when literally every cell of her distressed body had switched off. The Doctor was mesmerised and her poignant parting words will forever remain etched into my mind:

'Deep within all of us there is a fight, so powerful so strong, it can overcome any fear, any obstacle, any challenge. It can even intimidate and stave off death itself, even when death is at your doorstep staring you in the face, if your reason for living is big enough.'

Although the ambition to write a book was set years ago, the dreadful experience of hearing a dear loved one take their excruciatingly painful last breath, followed by the agonising and yet inspirational statement made by the Doctor was the crowning reason for turning my hankering to write, into a sturdy goal.

I'm enthralled by the concept of our capability to 'fight', against all conceived ideas and rationale, suggesting the human mind is blessed with an outstanding degree of power, arduous potential and a vigorous dynamism. Within all of us,

Motivation from a Tortured Mind

is the desire, enterprise and driving dexterity to achieve almost anything we want to: The majority of people on this earth live unfulfilled lives, never realising or understanding their gargantuan potential and leaving their lives to the democratic guarantee and dismal certainty of one day simply becoming dust or soil, having never witnessed the cunning adequacy they had sat dormant within their own head.

Life Options

Within the capabilities of every human there are three life options available:

1. Concede

2. Struggle

3. Fight.

1. **To concede** – is the acceptance of all you already are and everything you already have or the overall acknowledgement there is no need or method of achieving more. Materialistic, physical and emotional contentment. In many ways this is a wonderful situation, if you are truly satisfied and blissfully comfortable. What condition can be more gratifying than satisfaction and not having to think or work any harder because you've relinquished the desire of wanting or needing more than you already possess? The tragedy of knuckling under and conceding is when it's an unconditional defeatism based on the misunderstanding that there are mechanisms to greater achievement, of not knowing and understanding your personal capabilities, of not grasping the concept of your ticking time-bomb and the negligence of not realising the futility of time itself, with your forthcoming unpredictable and fatal conclusion, the assured transformation to dust or soil. Throughout the world there are many people who don't have the power and luxury of choice, they are forced to concede, there is no

option but to surrender and accept the dire circumstances they are encumbered with. For the remainder of humankind there is always a realistic and unanimous choice to not compromise or waive the opportunity and contingency of greater performance, triumph and accomplishment. Essentially almost everyone has the capacity to fight.

2. **To struggle** – Is the middle ground between the two extremes of not wanting to concede and actual attainment of the success you desire. A struggle can simply be a lack of direction, belief and tenacity or a distinct shortfall in skills, knowledge and experience to adequately fight. The majority of people categorically crave for greatness and abundance in their lives. Ask a million people if they desire more wealth, health and happiness and almost one hundred percent will be affirmative. Then ask them if they have the arrangement, structure and mechanism to achieve their personal nirvana and many will disappointingly say no, that they do not have the competent, satisfactory means or mental latitude to execute their ambitions. Multitudes of people struggle to reach their desired destinations and end up conceding and throwing in the towel or lowering their hopes and aspirations. To concede, isn't simply to surrender and accept what you have, it's a far greater incrimination than that, it's going through the struggle of trying and then abandoning, forlorn and defeated, the very things you had aspired to achieve. A struggle is a fight to win but one fraught with the dangers of failure and the dissolution from your endeavours. The difficult and crooked path to success, it can become too bothersome and inconvenient to continue, hence the reason why so many people finally concede. Learning to fight lessens the struggle and gives a greater affirmation of reaching the level of wealth, health and happiness you are aiming for.

3. **To fight** - Is to never concede, knowing that life is irritatingly and selfishly short and ill equipped to help those that aren't willing to help themselves. It's an ongoing altercation

to eke out every solitary ounce of joy from our limited days, to fiercely combat the negative attitudes, cynicism and discouragement of jaundiced, repugnant people. It's a daily confrontation with our personal reckoning of hope, vision and possibility and the insightful realisation they are integral to accomplish whatever is desired. It's a penetrating and conscious battle with anything that tries to corrupt, attack or pollute our personal belief, that we have the overriding command, to achieve whatever level of wealth, health and happiness we hunger for. Deep within all of us there is a fight, so powerful so strong, it can overcome any fear, any obstacle, any challenge and undoubtedly it will, it's power is undeniable, however in order to hammer and shape the life you want today there is a fundamental F.I.G.H.T you have to fully interpret, unconditionally adopt and instil deep into the essence of everything you undertake and every thought that transmits through your mind.

F.I.G.H.T

Fear

'The world enthusiastically but patiently awaits your awakening and the momentous shedding of your fearful skin that has cocooned you into a handicap of compliance, as your fearless wings develop, your flight will begin into a bright, sunshine engrossed sky of opportunity, a flight that will simply take you to places you hadn't dared to dream of, places that had been firmly ensconced in the unattainable distance, whilst you comfortably and without hesitation settled for second best'.

Fear is a powerful emotion induced by a perceived threat. There are many forms of fear and although they are entirely governed and instigated through our innate and acquired learning one particular form is a physical fear, a survival mechanism occurring in response to a specific stimulus such as pain or the threat of danger, it is the ability to recognise a hazardous, troublesome situation resulting in an urge to confront it or escape from it. Everyone has an instinctual response to potential threat and danger, this reaction is vitally important to the survival of all species and has been integral in the evolution of mankind. Fear is also directly related to certain behaviours of avoidance and escaping in reference to the perception of future events, where they are perceived as unacceptable or worsening, there's no doubt fear can also be triggered by something currently happening. Apart from fears that are physically treacherous there are a whole set of common fears, that many people suffer with for example, the existence of ghosts and evil powers, spiders, snakes, heights, water, enclosed spaces, bridges, tunnels, needles, public speaking the list is endless. These common fears are innate, cultural or inherited through the nurture of our lives and will forever be part of our society and there isn't always a necessity to overcome them unless they're strong enough to become counterproductive and debilitating, actually harming your very existence, diminishing the quality of your life or creating a barrier against what you want to achieve. Many people fear spiders but unless that fear is a total damnation upon your life resulting in a deterioration in your ability to function on a daily basis, there isn't really a huge need to combat the fear.

Fear – Peter & Jane

'Fear hems me in. I'm stitched into a corner.

It beats me, hurts me and stings every cell in my body.

I freeze, I die, it's killing me, I can't move.

But the fear is in my mind, it's created in my head, damn you fear, damn you.

If she cannot touch me she cannot harm me, if she cannot harm me, I cannot fear her.

How dare you enter my life, this is my Kingdom.

C'mon give me all you've got, I will make you fear me with my hatred of you.

Be gone and take all others with you.

I will be the monster, for my bravery will be the sword that takes your life.

This is my life and you cannot control it.

I have the strength.

I have the power to kill FEAR.'

That was an actual poem I wrote at the age of ten, under the powerful realisation that one has to conquer the fears that fill life with dread and trepidation, grasping the concept that dominating my psychological fear was the only way I could free my tortured mind of the decaying, cackling witch that sat on the edge of my bed, night after night, threatening to attack me.

Every ounce of input from the very moment we're born, via our five senses, has a direct or inadvertent impact on our lives. Overhearing my parents discuss witchcraft, black magic and sorcery clearly left an imprint upon my imagination and consciousness, one that reared it's unlikely, ugly head on many occasions throughout the course of my life.

Mum and Dad were clearly frightened themselves with the dark story passed on from an acquaintance of theirs, originating in their native India, the story of an evil ritual involving the casting of a deathly, crippling curse upon an unsuspecting person. An epitome of the sinful denunciation of good and reverence of satanic malevolence, causing untold anguish and mental harm to the recipient, cursing their life with the ghost of an evil, dead woman. The very same one that I'd now conjured to the edge of my bed. She would haunt every move of the person afflicted with her presence, filling their days with a scary, shadowy darkness, responsible for the evil miscarriages in their life, resulting in debauchery, murder and ultimately their untimely demise through a macabre suicide.

Every night my interpretation of that ridiculous story would make its presence felt, I could sense the cold, taunting vibration of evil in the room, resulting in horrific nightmares and endlessly sleepless nights. So painfully insomniac I was tempted to try Mum's sleeping tablets that I'd heard her mention so many times and the only reason I didn't was for the fear of being unable to wake as the evil witch attacked me, nevertheless those very sleeping pills were an act in rehearsal and would have their own poignant stage and role to play, later in life, particularly as their existence and effect had sparked my curiosity.

Peter and Jane were the insipid characters created to teach ten year olds how to recognise words, understand them and ultimately use them. They were key learning books for ten year olds throughout the land and a staple of the national school curriculum. I used to ponder about their unvarnished, vanilla existence. Their homely simple lives consisted of walking up a hill, opening a letter, throwing a ball, smelling a freshly baked pie and wearing striped pyjamas, a stark contradiction to the evilness positioned at the foot of my bed, waiting for me to sleep so she could gorge on my young face with her sharp, grey gravestone teeth. Many a time I wished for the mundane pleasures in life, of simply chasing a hoop down a hill, hiding under the kitchen table or just generally laughing for no reason at all, I craved the banality from the plain world of Peter & Jane. Their picture perfect innocuous world was my fantasy and formed the foundation for combating fear itself.

A daily input of prosaic, dull affirmations from Peter and Jane of how life should be for ten year olds, composed a monotonous world in my thoughtful imagination. Their colourless existence allowed me to imagine my life being lived with the same lacklustre happenings that they were living on a daily basis. The greater those images became the stronger my ability to dispute the atrocious evil resident in my bedroom. Using indiscriminate imagery from early learning literature, of humdrum lives and insignificant, dull circumstances I was becoming oblivious to my routine nightmares of evil.

To overcome a fear, one has to imagine a life without it, a presence that exists without, whatever the fear is. In time, as the fear of my witch depleted, her existence became inconsequential, until she finally disappeared for good.

To conclude, my ten year old season with the evil witch, was created through an overactive imagination, sparked and goaded with stories that I'd overheard my parents discussing. Then her demise was a consequence of imagining a life without her, conjured through the tenuous lives of fictional characters that appeared to live insubstantial but exceedingly happy lives. Nothing more than my own imagination, was the cause of that brief scary interlude and ultimately its destruction.

Fear – The Vows

'I, Rebecca, take you Michael, to be my lawfully wedded husband, to have and to hold, from this day forward, for better, for worse, for richer, for poorer, in sickness and in health, until death do us part.'

As per usual hearing wedding vows always tug the romantic heart strings within me and evoke pleasant emotions, usually resulting in gleeful tears, it was no different at Rebecca and Michael's wedding. I'd known Rebecca for many years and throughout those years she had been through a tirade of failed, unhappy relationships, so to see her on her wedding day, so beautiful in her wedding dress and hear her take her wedding vows was heart warming and blissfully emotional.

It's the final touching words *'until death do us part'* that the dreamy, sentimental part of me finds most endearing and adorable. The mere fact that someone is committing the entirety of their life to the person that is stood in front of them, that this is it, this is the final person they will be devoted to, until death itself parts them. There is nothing on this entire planet more meaningful or considerable than devoting one's life to another and stating it'll stay that way until the grim reaper scythes life into oblivion. It's no wonder that I helplessly blubber at that significant moment when someone's intention is to pledge the rest of their days to another.

'I'm so pleased for you Rebecca, I never thought I'd hear you say those words, until death do us part, that you've finally found someone to spend the rest of your life with.'

'Rest of my life, what you mean with Michael, are you bloody crazy?'

Taken aback by Rebecca's vitriolic retort, I instantly assumed it was her nerves, after all this was the biggest day of her entire life.

'I mean, I just want you to know how happy I am that you've found someone you're so happy to be with and someone that will be by your side forever, until one of you dies.'

'You are bloody crazy. I'm not going to be with Michael for the rest of my life, I married Michael just in case there isn't someone else. I'm thirty three years old, I feared not meeting the right person, I feared spending my days alone, I feared not being married, I feared that I'd never fall in love and live happily ever after.'

This crushing dialogue between Rebecca and I happened on an actual wedding day, before the bride had even taken her beautiful ivory wedding dress off.

In reality, Rebecca was willing to get married to Michael because of the burgeoning threat of fear that was surrounding her. Fear that she would be alone and the fear that deep, passionate romance and love doesn't really exist and that she would just spend her entire life searching for it, instead it was easier to be with Michael because it alleviated the fears that were otherwise hounding her. In other words she accepted a second best existence, just in case the life she dreamed of didn't happen.

Building a relationship with or even getting married to the wrong person unknowingly is acceptable it's a heady part of our growth and development and part of this adventure called life we're unwittingly slung into. Naturally, there are times when people enter into second best relationships that over time develop into lifelong romances fulfilling mutual needs of companionship, desire and love. However, knowingly jeopardising your rightful constitution for happiness by letting fear reign over your life is fundamentally flawed and misguided.

Rebecca's sentiments and behaviour were not unusual. Fear of the unknown has a tendency to encourage haphazard leaps and bounds in life and often compromising what we really desire. Fear alone can endanger our chances of discovering true fulfilment and a truly contented life.

The controlling force of fear is by no means restricted to love, marriage and relationships, the very same debilitations apply to almost every area of your life that involves the power of choice. Often we're falsely imprisoned by the inherent limitations of fear and make choices and take actions because fear whispers those little binding phrases into our ears *'this is it, there is no better', 'this is your last chance', 'you'll never do better than this', 'you're thirty three, that's getting old'* and so on.

Many of our fears are manifested through our own insecurities in our ability to do better or possess more than we have, they're self-fulfilling parodies of our own attitudes and low self-esteem. Fear becomes us when we're lacking confidence in our finesse to accomplish the contentment we absolutely crave, hence we settle for easier victories and achievements that have a lower chance of failure, these are unlikely to be the real things we hungered for, so by default we've settled for an unsatisfactory second best and have directly shrunk our dreams by cowering from our resident, inherent fears.

Fear will hem you into a box, restrict your movement and slow your personal development, you may see a glimmer of light when you crane your neck and look up, you may even stretch out and reach the lid of your cramping four walls but you'll never quite escape its irrevocable confinement. Outside of your mental incarceration is a world desperately crying out to be vanquished, a world that will willingly accept defeat and hand over to you its sparkling, invaluable crown jewels, the one way ticket to first place, to you heralding championship and achieving first-best, the precise position you doubtlessly wanted to be in but amenably ignored, brushed aside for fear of failure. Between you and that promised land of assured personal gratification are your four-walls of fear, strengthened on a daily basis by your acceptance and worship of fear itself, empowered and fortified by the weighty threat of potential disappointment, perceived inadequacy and the insecurity of rejection.

The world enthusiastically but patiently awaits your awakening and the momentous shedding of your fearful skin that has cocooned you into a handicap of compliance, as your fearless wings develop, your flight will begin into a bright, sunshine engrossed sky of opportunity, a flight that will simply take you to places you hadn't dared to dream of, places that had been firmly ensconced in the unattainable distance, whilst you comfortably and without hesitation settled for second best.

1. Imagining and living a world void of the fear that is bludgeoning and controlling your existence is paramount in overcoming it and significantly moving on. The 'Peter & Jane effect' can be utilised in almost any situation, the key is imagination and understanding precisely how it would physically and mentally feel without that caustic

fear holding you back. That includes all the associated emotions of happiness, relief and elation of shaking the fear or of it never existing in the first place. This thinking process creates positive affirmations, which conjure the strength to lessen the significance of the fear itself and like the cackling witch on my bed, the fear may still exist but its effect is minimal and meaningless, therefore ineffective in your life. There is no fear that cannot be controlled and overcome with the immense power of imagination. There is no need to concede to it or struggle with it and every reason to fight it.

2. Confront your fears with the deafening noise from your ticking time-bomb. It lives, breathes and ticks inside your head. Each second that passes is a second closer to the almighty explosion just waiting to happen, just waiting to conclude your life and say a final farewell to all that vision, hope and possibility that you were blessed with. Time is clearly your enemy but an enemy that will gladly join forces with you and tackle the oncoming evil, relentless army of fear. A gargantuan barrier against the fear brigade, it will aggressively resist fear's intentions and reinforce your backbone, which fear readily attacks, buckles and forces submission, leaving you weary, forlorn and defeated. The onset of time and your ticking time-bomb is a powerful weapon of mass destruction against the life crumpling and resolve weakening effect of your fears.

3. Accept there will be fears borne of the life you've already lived, many of them subconsciously and subliminally created. We are all the result of absolutely every miniscule thing we've ever heard, witnessed and done. Every corner turned, every breath taken, every thought transmitted has circumvented our lives to this moment now. Through that immense roller-coaster, breathtaking journey, we've observed and gleaned a ponderous collection of emotions. Some of them have fabricated our insecurities, uncertainties and fears. Remembering and realising some of our key

conscious happenings is often the first step to conquering some of the fears we're burdened with. Whether they're bed-ridden witches created from overheard stories or counterproductive statements from our protective parents telling us that becoming an astronaut is impossible, they are all rooted somewhere in our past and each and every one of them is unquestionably conquerable, once their origins are ascertained.

4. Use and manipulate your fears to fuel and generate your ambitions. Rather than fear holding you back it can actually be an authoritarian catalyst, guiding and bolstering your desires. A compelling enforcement it can create a benchmark emotional perception of how you may feel disappointment, failure and dejection if you fail to acquire the aspirations you strive for. Transport yourself into the future and conceptualise pictures and images of your life, void of all the elements you are dreaming of today. A life without your dream house could be an example of a provocative fear, which could result in remaining where you are today, or worse in an undesirable residential location and home. Undoubtedly there are amazing destinations around the globe that you've always wanted to visit, the Taj Mahal in India, The Great Wall of China, The Inca Trail in Peru, the Pyramids of Giza, the Statue of Liberty in New York, countless awe-inspiring cities, countries, monuments and beautiful sights that conjure magical emotions of exploration, learning and adventure, that have featured in your thoughts and imagination. Now execute the unrelenting influence of fear and imagine the possibility of never witnessing the marvels of the world you've envisaged and dreamt about. That quelling notion, deep feeling of regretful failing that you could live a life and never, ever fulfil your habitual hankering to experience the world, should be the foundation on which you can strategically build your plans, if travel is on the itinerary and agenda of your life.

5. Fear lowers your threshold to pain, therefore when confronted with whatever it is you fear, naturally your

emotional and physical ability to withstand the showdown is substantially lower than someone that doesn't have that particular fear. One of the most pertinent stabbing, knife twisting vulnerabilities of fear, is the fear of rejection. A dismissal of anything we truly believe in from love and relationships to business proposals and religion affects our psyche and in many situations affects our self-esteem, spirit and dignity, often leaving a feeling of lowered morale, despair and in extreme cases gloomy depression. Renunciation in our individual beliefs is commonplace, even when executed by those dear to our lives. However no matter how customary and systematic the rejections are, they still affect us to the core of our subconscious and essence of life. Focused concentration on our hopes, vision and possibilities, that create our dominant inspirations is the most competent and convincing armoury to defend and protect ourselves to such a millstone of human behaviour. Inspiration is undoubtedly the key.

Inspiration

'Without an element of inspiration the continual improvement and evolvement of life would come to a grinding halt and probably cease to exist. Inspiration delivers the reasons why, which are a foundational cornerstone and integral building block of everything on the human agenda of existence.'

The divine influence and cerebral power that elevates, stimulates, empowers, and awakens the senses, creating an exertion of enthusiasm, encouragement and illumination of the mind and soul. An overpowering energetic motivation, a potent stimulus that leverages action, alertness and immense command enabling one to undertake physical and emotional accomplishments with fluidity and ease. Inspiration is the magnetically encouraging and lustrously glowing beacon, forever shining its guiding light upon every journey that evolves from an innermost heartfelt location.

Everyone has an alternative definition and personalised catalogue of inspiration. From people, parents, children, religion, history, achievements, family, books, drawings, quotes to poetry and life itself the list of where inspiration is derived from is endless. The list of success, creativity and results achieved through being inspired is an equally unquenchable list. Without an element of inspiration the continual improvement and evolvement of life would come to a grinding halt and probably cease to exist. Inspiration delivers the reasons why, which are a foundational cornerstone and integral building block of everything on the human agenda of existence. Inspiration bolsters motivation, attitude, belief, hope, vision and possibility, it fuels and fertilises growth in every aspect of personal development and performance.

Inspiration has led me from consummate failure and life's general shenanigans to immense successes and every exhilarating twist and turn in-between. Either way it never failed to deliver. I was inspired with hope, vision and possibility with the monumental sight restoring words *'Deep, deep inside your heart you have to believe you will see again. Even if you only have one tiny ounce of hope left that one day your sight will return, then you need to hang onto that because that one ounce of hope will get you through, that single ounce will give you a reason to live. Sometimes all you need is hope'* That inspiring sentence instilled a twinkle of hope that ultimately helped me survive through one of the darkest episodes in my life. Consequently, that string of events set the inspiration and inception of writing this book, which was then further stimulated by Mum's gargantuan fight to stay alive, encapsulated and immortalised by the inspirational words from her nurse *'Deep within all of us there is a fight, so powerful so strong, it can overcome any fear, any obstacle, any challenge. It can even intimidate and stave off death itself, even when death is at your doorstep staring you in the face, if your reason for living is big enough'* Which not only inspired some of the content of 'Motivation from a tortured Mind' but gave me that final propulsion and impetus I desperately needed to get it started.

Inspiration - Somchai

The intense heat and relentless, burning sun were searing and prickling my skin, I was hot, uncomfortable and intimidated, it was 42c in the busiest, most hectic, animated, disorderly and frenzied city on earth, Bangkok, capital of Thailand. With over eight million inhabitants, it seemed like they were all bustling, pushing and shouting on the very overcrowded pavement that I was desperately trying to navigate through. Naturally with my chunky, western build and culturally different features to the Thai people I was everything between an amusing novelty and a curious circus oddity, particularly as this was a more rural area of Bangkok, lesser frequented by foreign aliens such as myself, I stood out like a huge rabbit surrounded by thousands of mice, wondering what business I had being there, where I clearly didn't belong. Avoiding a particularly feisty throng of frenetic Thais clamouring towards me, I moved closer to the shop rather than the road, which had a whirlwind of crazily driven cars, bikes and anything else that had wheels on it, careering around uncontrollably and just looked far too dangerous to step into. I stared with nonchalance at the tacky, fake looking jewellery on display in the dusty shop window. My throat was dry as sandpaper and my patience wearing desperately thin, when I felt a feeble, yet due to my heightened awareness, alarming tug on my trousers. I physically recoiled, swiftly freeing myself of the hand that had dared to touch me. Instantaneously as my melodramatic rebound action, the portly, red-faced sweating shop-keeper came trundling out of his shop, brandishing what can only be described as a stick the size and weight of a cricket bat. Images of explaining my wounds and the embarrassment of a street beating with an audience of thousands of oriental mice laughing at the huge rabbit victim, rapidly swept through my mind, causing an involuntary defensive stance of shrieking and sticking my arms out in an odd quivering fashion, in order to limit the carnage I was about to endure. Before I could even attempt to hop away from my enraged assailant, he forcefully, using the large girth of his body bulldozed me out of the way, turned his back on me and whilst shouting ferocious, hateful sounding obscenities commenced bashing the owner of the hand that had tugged at my trousers. After administering the abrupt and numerous blows to his arms, shoulders, head and back, the shop-keeper turned to me and with a softer tone of voice and in his broken, pigeon English muttered an apology on behalf of the casualty he had just mercilessly battered *'sorry mister he no longer touch you, please come buy from my shop'* I was in utter disbelief and shock, although I'd just been heroically saved from an innocent tug of the trousers, I wasn't about to show my gratitude and step into his shop. I just nervously backed off, turned around and went scuttling back to my hotel. What followed was a desperately thoughtful and melancholy evening. I was plagued with images of the rampant beating dished out by the fat shopkeeper. The repentant screaming of the unlucky victim was ferociously ringing in my ears, as was the grisly battering noise made by the cricket bat like weapon, as it fiercely struck his head and cracked against his skull, drowning out his desperate pleas for the shopkeeper to stop.

The anxious evening transposed into an unwelcome vicious nightmare, the shopkeeper had metamorphosed into Satan himself and I was at the mercy of his vitriolic violence but being the ill-fated owner of an ominous tortured mind, I wasn't merely receiving a physical lambasting from the devil, he was also for added drama, eating my flesh as vulgar scurrying cockroaches feasted on the bloody remains.

A simple journey, albeit in a frenetic place and now I was having vile nightmares and carrying the cumbersome burden of knowing I instigated an unnecessary thrashing upon someone who dared to touch my leg. There was only one way to relieve my degraded conscience, I needed to find the victim and somehow compensate him for the disgraceful assault he endured.

Stepping out of the luxury hotel, I was once again embroiled in the delirious and unbalanced, sweltering metropolis that is Bangkok. The heat was oppressive and intolerable as was the reaction of the locals, as I provocatively stepped into their world, from the decadence and extravagance of my air-conditioned residence. From the deep red carpet of the stunning hotel lobby to the cockroach, ridden bedraggled street, the disparity was immeasurable and the two contrasting worlds were literally and disturbingly side by side. The cost of the breakfast I had no appetite to eat and had just left on the table could have probably fed one of these dishevelled communities for weeks. Irony abound, I only needed to take a few cautious steps, avoiding beggars, insects and squalor before I saw the shopkeeper's victim whose fateful encounter had plagued my selfish existence for twenty four hours.

I enthusiastically crossed the road, avoiding every known vehicle to man from bikes and mules to humongous tankers and of course cars, all of them being driven precariously and at breakneck speeds, almost as if myself and anyone else crossing was completely invisible. Trundling over to him, I wondered why he was still laying on the pavement and a frightening thought crossed my already agitated mind, maybe the shopkeeper had inflicted permanent damage and insufferable pain upon him, hence he was languishing in agony, unable to stand up. He was positioned on his stomach staring at the pavement, furiously pursing his dry, cracked lips and blowing at the dusty concrete, to my horror his bizarre action wasn't deranged as it first appeared, he was blowing to keep a repulsive shiny, black beetle, the shape of a ladybird but the size of an adult thumb, from hungrily approaching his face. In the utter confusion and distraction of the moment I swiftly pushed the wretched insect aside with my foot and it scurried away.

There were hundreds of people scampering around on this grubby pavement, why didn't anyone notice, considering they were actually stepping over him, that this man with a blood stained bandage around his head was on the floor and worse still trying to avoid a deadly looking beetle from attacking his face? He craned his neck to look up at me and smiled with an awkward nod, acknowledging that I'd saved him from having his face eaten. Instinctively, I bent down, even though the unwashed stench from him was intolerable and grasped his arm to help him stand up, I quickly let go as he ferociously shook his head. Having felt his hapless, bony arm, I guessed my clench was too strong for his vulnerable frame. At that point upon straightening my own less than vulnerable frame, the full horror and distress hit me in the face like a full frontal collision with one of the careering tankers. An instant wave of depression washed over very single cell of my already sweat drenched body. There were no legs in his trousers. From mid-thigh downwards it was just cloth, this street vagrant, was hopelessly lying on his stomach because he had no legs to get up with, let alone to walk with. I was in utter shock at this sight of human degradation, a man barely alive having lived through a callous cricket bat attack, head still bleeding from the ensuing wounds was stretching his arms out on the pavement and with the feeble strength in his fingertips living and moving his body along the filth, insects and ignorant, couldn't care less feet of thousands of passers-by, to whom he was nothing more than a burdensome inconvenience. This was the epitome of a crazed, degrading and depraved society. A prejudiced, criminal world where a man who scrapes his beaten frame along the pavement, blowing away beetles and cockroaches that eagerly want to feast on his brain by burrowing through his eyes, is spared his vision only to see the magnificent lifestyle represented by the hotel I was staying in, where I recall leaving a breakfast worth more money than this wretch will ever see in his miserable, tainted life. My emotional strength buckled and symbolically brought me to my knees, as if life wasn't harsh enough for this cripple, I'd incited superfluous pain upon him, through my jittery reaction when he touched my leg no more than twenty four hours ago. The woeful dramatisation in my mind, replaying the beating, was an inconsolable stab deep in my heart. It was tearing my sanity to shreds and forming uncontrollable tears in my eyes. Without another thought I reached into my pocket and handed him a thousand Baht note, priceless to him, worth about fifteen pounds sterling, he cried in disbelief as tears flowed down the crumpled ingrained deep tracks in his skin that probably all had an individual sorrowful tale to tell of a torn, downbeat existence, worthless and pointless. He wetted the pavement with his crying as insects dashed over the dampness and darted under his lame body.

Placing the screwed up thousand Baht note into the pocket of his half-filled trousers, he grabbed my leg and pointed to the alley next to where we were and started to scrape his way into it, beckoning me to follow, much to the displeasure of any bystanders caring to notice.

The alley was dark and dubious with a pungent aroma of cooking food laced with the vile smell of stale urine. There were dogs barking and kids irrepressibly running around, with people sat in doorways staring with equal measures of contempt, wonder and distrust. He scraped his body through puddles, grime and faeces until we turned into a doorway, which was clearly the kitchen area of a restaurant, there was acrid steam rising from the boiling pots of food as cooks in soiled, greasy clothes shouted at each other. Through the kitchen we entered a dimly lit room, no bigger than a small garden shed, in the corner was an old woman just rocking to & fro, there were other people just lying around, I counted seven others, cramped into this hot, stinking hell hole, in the back of an insect infested kitchen. This obscene dump of human beings was clearly his home. From within the throng of inhabitants a little girl no older than ten years of age appeared, her left leg was bandaged as she slowly limped closer. The crippled man started a warbling conversation with her. She looked at me with her large sad eyes that no doubt had witnessed more sorrow than a child should ever be exposed to. Her face was covered in repulsive sores and her lips could barely move, they were painfully swollen but she croaked out a sentence in broken English *'my father is happy, you friend, you stay here'.*

This was the beginning of a twenty minute conversation in which his daughter was the quirky translator. The cripple was named Somchai, he lived in this disgusting squalor with nine other people and thousands of crawling, filthy cockroaches, including his mentally deranged Mother who was rocking in the corner. Apsara, the nine year old translator had a mutilating disease which was gradually destroying her limbs, it seemed to be irrational normality that she was unlikely to survive another year, just because they couldn't afford the necessary medication. Somchai's legs were amputated when he was in a calamitous car crash, colliding head on with a tanker, the catastrophic encounter catapulted his car into the air and it landed on its roof, trapping him inside the tangled mess. They cut his legs because it was easier than rescuing him from the wreckage. He never had the opportunity to consider the potential of hope, vision and possibility, the emergency services sliced his body apart without a second thought. Any compensation that should have been awarded due to the haphazard driving of the tanker driver was invalid because it was deemed the dismembering wasn't necessary, the Doctor on location insisted to the court that Somchai had given his permission for the amputation. Somchai wasn't even consulted and can recall the grinding vibration that seared through his body as the saw cut through his bones, he was too weak and delirious to protest and simply watched the gruesome drama unfold and lay there hoping it all to be a sordidly, wicked nightmare from which he was about to wake.

Desperate indignity, foul diseases, a pointless dejected existence and absolutely zero belief in anything tangible but a solid underlying determination to survive against all the odds. Their lives and the vitriolic rain that has drenched their days has without doubt inspired me to live, work and fight through all the obstacles that have dared to attack, slow and adversely affect my life, futile happenings that pale into insignificance in comparison to the defilement Somchai and Apsara referred to as life.

Benevolence and gratitude encourage soul stirring endearment, however the immeasurable indebtedness demonstrated by Somchai and his family, for the limited humanity I was able to offer, was totally disproportionate. The world we live in has millions of people superfluously suffering, not just through famine and impoverishment but through corrupt political regimes, natural disasters and debased economies, such contamination of humankind, contravening our god-given right to live happy, contented, healthy fruitful lives are rife on this unbalanced Earth. The media rightly so, avidly report the disenchantment and jaundice of our cruel, unpredictable and treacherous world, creating compassion and numerous humanitarian operations that assist people, communities and entire countries with deserved philanthropic attention. The difference in Bangkok was my chance encounter with such a degenerate existence was totally unexpected, I was embroiled within it and the people concerned were not asking for humanity or even sympathy, this wasn't a huge explosive media revelation, begging people to show charity, on the contrary I'd actually crow-barred myself into their lives. My confrontation with misfortune and mishaps of an embittered world shook my conscience with a bloodthirsty vengeance, boldly questioning my own life with a razor sharp perspective.

Our relationship during that particular visit to Bangkok and the further two jaunts I made over the following eighteen months was symbiotically valuable. A priceless connection is created when both sides of a friendship benefit from the fusion, both being affected in a positive manner. For Somchai and his family I provided elementary subsistence no more costly than a week of decadent breakfast's that I usually didn't eat, this afforded them a rudimentary upgrade in their standard of living and an enhancement of their dreary reality. In return the relationship was more parasitic than symbiotic, my personal gain from the heartfelt Bangkok liaison was monumental and a lifelong lesson of inspiration, far greater in substance, definition and personal gratification than the cost of a few breakfast's.

In 2009, I heard the devastating news that Apsara died from the crippling disease that her pre-teenage body was saddled with, another wasted young life in this unreasonable world and yet she would always find an illuminating smile through the constant pain and discomfort and despite living a downtrodden, destitute life, surrounded by the manipulative scum on the evil, relentless streets of Bangkok, her attitude to a life, that was gradually slipping away was eternally optimistic. I recall her taking me by the hand and helplessly hobbling through a dingy alley, just to show me where she often sat and watched the sun go down, it was an incredible sight, which gave an air of reverence to an almost irrelevant, penniless, ailing existence.

Almost a year later Somchai also suffered a tragic demise, he died from an appalling head wound, it's not clear how the catastrophe actually happened, however the English speaking Indian waiter that I'd commissioned, to watch over the hapless family, wrote me the following melancholy letter.

Dear Mr Khatkar

I bring you sad news. Somchai died yesterday. He had a bruise on his head but could not remember how it happened, he was very sick, so I took him to hospital, I sat with him for two hours then he died. The Doctor said Somchai had a cracked skull and internal bleeding. Somchai asked me to write to you and say thank you friend, for what you did and he also wanted to answer your question that you asked him when you first went to his house, he just wanted you to know. He said 'everything from the day, the night, the sun to the rain. I respect I've had life, I respect that even without legs I still had life, I would die a thousand painful deaths to just live for one day. Apsara was sick but smiled every day and every smile made all my pain go away. Apsara died but her memory made me live. Whatever one suffers, as long as there is still breath left it's all worth it. Sleep little my friend, live and laugh very much and find yourself strong reasons that mean everything, reasons you breathe for, this will be your song, then every day you will sing your own song and you will live a life of achievement, satisfaction and passion'.

Goodbye for now Mr Khatkar, I will post you the necklace that belonged to Apsara. Somchai wanted you to have it.

Inderjit Phal

The question I had nonchalantly asked Somchai, upon hearing about the horrendous circumstances surrounding his accident and witnessing where he and his family lived, was quite simply *'what inspires you',* I was intrigued, bewildered and mesmerised at the outstanding stalwart attitude that Somchai and Apsara were blessed with, their reluctance to let their impoverished, drained lives wipe the smiles from their permanently, impaired faces and destroy the fighting philosophies they had in abundance, were nothing short of heroically amazing. He didn't answer at the time, as his demented Mother had started shouting and fiercely slapping her own head and Apsara needed to leave our three-way conversation and tend to her.

Somchai's story and the letter from the waiter forever serves as a catalyst to stir my own personal inspiration, often when my life has revolved around some insignificant occurrence, I remember the turmoil, poverty and abasement that Somchai suffered every day of his arduous life, which acutely shines a blinding light of perspective directly onto my own challenges. In comparison my issues always appear so hollow and futile. Somchai never had long-term ambitions or goals, as every waking day was a goal within itself, a goal to survive and provide what he could for his indisposed family. That commendable measure by which each day was accounted for, made merely staying alive an exemplary mission, it provided a monumental reason why, that was powered by the desire to fulfil the obligations of his family and the domineering fear that without him they would be abandoned and at the mercy of a cruel and overwhelming city.

The most everlasting lesson from my friend in Bangkok was simply the closing line of his message, minutes before he took his mournful final breath *'find yourself strong reasons that mean everything, reasons you breathe for, this will be your song, then every day you will sing your own song and you will live a life of achievement, satisfaction and passion'.*

Goals

'Your goals are what should inspire you to go to extraordinary lengths, have unlimited stamina and the strength to withstand all the disgraceful negative stones the world will bludgeon you with because they don't have the harmony, power, determination and success of their own song.'

Resonating deep within every miniscule cell of flesh, blood and bones a vibration so intensely disturbing that the pounding melee quakes the heart into absolute submission and gushes the brain with a torrent of altercating discord and fanatical, headstrong emotions. Bulldozing rationality and impartiality into a stimulating path upon which hazards, obstacles and challenges are swept away with the strength, durability and tenacity of the hypnotic, alluring and commanding bellow known as 'your song'. It makes time, it creates time as it mesmerises your entirety into a focused regime of daily, weekly and monthly actions, ones which breathe life into the words that make up that most desirable entity. Your song is the driving, pushing, jostling force that shines an incandescent beam through the murky mist and debilitating, conventional fog that surrounds us. Your song reverberates through the daily rigmarole which inadvertently drags our lives into a habitual existence. Your song quite simply is your reason why. Your song is your inspiration, the very impetus that inspires a plan, mindset, attitude and gusto to achieve it. But it must all begin with a song, your song.

'Find yourself strong reasons that mean everything, reasons you breathe for, this will be your song, then every day you will sing your own song and you will live a life of achievement, satisfaction and passion.'

Whatever you passionately want, unconditionally need and desperately desire must press the right emotional buttons deep within you, which then trigger a volcanic response to your senses. Every sense you are blessed with is heightened and ready to work to the tune of your song, singing it's gracious, longing harmony in everything you do. Your eyes set the vision in all you can see. Every sight is a hindrance or reminder of your song. Your ears tune into the harmonies that linger in all your thoughts, each and every one echoing the tune you yearn for. The smell of success hangs over you like a glorious, sugary fluffy cloud, knowing that every day you physically touch and tempt your song closer with the defined actions from your plan to achieve it. Every accomplishment on your unbridled path gives you another sweet taste of your song coming to fruition, blooming and tantalising your taste buds until they explode with desire and the anticipation of reaching your destination.

Your song is your personal inspiration, embedded deep within your mindset and in your sight. It's a crazed yearning, omnipotent in all you undertake, unrelenting in its provocation, rewarding by its mere presence and alliance with your desire, significant without exception, in every corner of your mind and your very existence. Emotionally overwhelming with its power, tenacity and fortitude, it becomes a necessary part of your life. This is your song. If your goals sing 'Your Song', there is little that's unachievable and throughout the course of history nothing substantial has ever been achieved without the stirring of these authoritative and efficacious impassioned emotions.

Y	Yearning

O	Omnipotent

U	Unrelenting

R	Rewarding

S	Significant

O	Overwhelming

N	Necessary

G	Goals

Goals and goal setting are undoubtedly among the most written about, taught and trained personal growth and development philosophies and still remain generally misunderstood and incompetent in assisting people reach their personal objectives. The fundamental flaw in basic goal setting that is a major provocation inciting failure and ultimately dooming an attempt to fulfil goals is summed up in the line that Somchai wrote in the closing statement of his letter 'Find yourself strong reasons that mean everything, reasons you breathe for.' uncompromising and poignant, it doesn't relate to anything less than earth shattering, commanding, electrifying reasons that form the foundation of your goals, reasons that will naturally be an encroachment upon your comfort zone and propel you to stretch harder and higher than you could ever have imagined. Locating 'your song' is the most difficult and yet most exceptional part of setting and achieving goals. The unquestionable root cause of not accomplishing anything substantial is the inability in discovering 'your song', without such an impulse beating and resonating through your veins, every challenge, every obstacle, every discerning negative person along your path represents a daunting, un-scalable mountain, which undeniably results in changing course, settling for second best or surrendering entirely.

If 'Your Song' is the decisive stimulus that propagates the purpose, execution and fulfilment of your goals, then it's no wonder Somchai concluded '*you will live a life of achievement, satisfaction and passion*'.

Any goal, lifetime ambition or target will drive a stake of desire straight through your heart, if it is fuelled and powered by 'your song', if your current goals don't incite these potent, breathtaking emotions then they're not worth the paper they're written on. It's clearly the difference between flying over the ocean to reach your destination in an aeroplane or trying to get there in a rowing boat. Of course there's a slim chance the boat would make it, however the journey would be tiresome, treacherous, disheartening and time consuming with a massive likelihood of complete failure or settlement for the dreaded second best.

1. Are your goals inspiring you and singing 'your song'? Does the thought of achieving them play an enchanting melody in your mind, leaving you mesmerised and in a hypnotic trance, particularly knowing the consuming emotions that will surge through you, invigorating and awakening every cell of your body, when you achieve them? If not, then either your goals are insubstantial or worse, they're not your true desires and dreams.

2. Every day 'your song' will sing to you as you open your eyes in the morning, throughout the entirety of the day and as you close your eyes to sleep. All worthwhile goals are represented by a burning, searing desire to achieve them and the very thought of failure saddles you with an unequivocal fear, almost an unimaginable, heart-sinking scenario of not having what 'your song' represents.

3. Everyone has a song, identifying your song is a talent. One has to think without restriction, imagine without boundaries and let the power of curiosity and the damned ticking time bomb in our heads be the catalysts to discover the magical nirvana we all crave. Tragically most of us hugely underachieve, never realising the beautiful ambrosia of life is within our grasp and that we have

the potential to attain it. Our song doesn't prevail, not a single note is played, pitifully silenced by our ineptitude to accept magnanimous achievements are within our realms, if only we could free ourselves from the shackles of mediocre thinking, borne through years of meeting oppressive, malignant personalities for whom the world is a burden, not a powerful resource that when aligned with heart-stopping goals, delivers without fail, instead we busy ourselves chasing meaningless, easily achieved soporific goals, which in reality don't even deserve the accolade of being called 'goals'.

Inspiration is available in abundance 'your song' will inspire you to fly without wings, to your desired purpose, destination and objective. That power is dormant and waiting like an immense grand piano, which with focused and talented fingers, fortitude and the desire to play your song will produce an everlasting tune that will ring its beautiful melody within your ears and throughout your life, long after you've accomplished your song.

Your goals are what should inspire you to go to extraordinary lengths, have unlimited stamina and the strength to withstand all the disgraceful negative stones the world will bludgeon you with because they don't have the harmony, power, determination and success of their own song.

Goals - My Song

The gentle strumming of my song had been tunefully present for years and years now but was it really 'my song'? A goal that can be described as a yearning, omnipotent, unrelenting, rewarding, significant, overwhelming, necessary goal should have been a deafening rock concert in my head, not a gentle, listless strumming. Anything quieter than a restless, thrashing, obstreperous guitar was hardly capable of motivating any form of action, therefore by default was nothing more than a wanton wish, a flimsy dream, a wishy-washy, languid idea. It was a 'one-day wonder', 'one-day I'll do it, one-day I'll get there, one-day my dreams will come true'. The precise 'one-day' that irrefutably never arrives and has the uncanny potential of constituting part of your regret portfolio, once the lethal ticking time-bomb within your head is detonated.

Everyone has songs playing in their minds, writing a book was one of mine. These wanton wishes are our escape from the routine, mediocre existences many of us are embroiled in. We constantly dream of the house we'd like to live in, the car we would like to drive or the dream destination we'd like to holiday in. It's those lucid, escapism dreams that can develop a song, into 'your song'. The one that will convert from an apathetic, drowsy ditty to a synchronised symphony of sound, vociferous in every waking moment, one you're passionate and compelled to achieve.

What is the intriguing process that incites the monumental development of a wanton wish into a soaring, bellowing, craving goal? How and when does a seedling note, that's nonchalantly playing an innocuous tune within the many corridors of our convoluted minds, transform into a cacophony of noise, performing at the very forefront of our awareness? A noise so emphatic it inspires the impulse, vitality and procedure to execute whatever is required to manage and manipulate the cerebral pandemonium, ultimately metamorphosing the goal into an everyday reality.

Goals - Motivation from a Tortured Mind

'There is a spark of magic inside everyone. The tragedy of life is most people never realise their true potential, they live and die without ever turning that spark into a flame. Find your magic spark. It will turn your life into an unforgettable adventure, a bright, eternal flame that will live on much longer than you do. Live your life and set the world on fire.'

These were the immortal words inscribed above the blackboard in the English department where I studied. Formidable in their sentiment and powerful in their guidance, attempting to deter the students from the humdrum path of mediocrity that most people are forced to tread.

My intensely academic and profound English Literature lecturer would, almost at the beginning of every lecture, take the classroom statement one step further. With a certain air of contempt and nonconformity she would peer over her glasses and croakily address the students.

'Yes, there is a spark in all of you. Yes, you should all have an adventure. Yes, you should all set the world on fire. However, I want you to remember your life is a book. No matter what you do, where you go or what you become put your book onto paper. The tragedy of life is that everyone has a book within them but they never get to tell their story, for it is that story that has the potential of setting the world on fire.'

At the beginning of almost every session for two years, she would repeat those enlightened, heartfelt words. It became the predictable start to every English Literature lecture. On my last day, as I went to thank her for the effort and determination she had consistently demonstrated, not to mention the immense knowledge she imparted, making literature and poetry so accessible, influential and understandable, I asked the double-barrel question that had haunted me for almost the two years that she had lectured us *'does everyone really have a book within them and where's yours'* Her eminent answer became the embodiment and foundation stone of my personal quest to put words onto paper.

'You don't need to raise the Titanic, climb Mount Everest or be a powerful millionaire. Your book is not about fame and fortune, your book is in your heart. It's a personal representation of your life. Everything you do, everything you experience will be meaningful in some way or another to someone. Whatever your book is, don't leave it unwritten and always tell everyone you know, that they too have a book within them. In ten years no student has asked me about mine, about my book. The answer is simple, that's the tragedy of my life. I haven't yet told my story. Nevertheless, one day I will put pen to paper.'

It took the manifestation of landmark, majestic and noteworthy developments and inspiration through the course of my life for its ambitious transformation into words, everything from blindness, accidents and grievous heartbreak to the multitude of people that have coloured, shaded and influenced my heady journey. Nevertheless, its our experiences and heartfelt passion that build the foundation, structure and sustainability of our goals.

The tune of my song had its first notes played by a remarkably persistent English lecturer, the melody and song nurtured from that diminutive seedling, creating an ear-piercing symphony orchestra, triumphantly blaring out my harmony. By day lyrically binding every step I took, by night keeping me awake with its incessant bellowing, I wholeheartedly understood the power of having a goal, from the noise it created in my life but it still needed a beginning, a reason an end and ultimately a solid, workable plan. 'Motivation from a Tortured Mind' was not about to bloom with passion and good intentions alone. The song in my ears needed to become a physical entity in my life, a stratagem I could actualise, one that would manacle my passion and purpose and generate an actual incarnate result.

Goals – Six vital steps

1. Your Song – Yearning, Omnipotent, Unrelenting, Rewarding, Significant, Overwhelming, Necessary Goals are deep within you, your song is waiting to be discovered, just lingering to enliven your life with its alluring sound. Lift the blanket of self doubt, low self-esteem and fear that is protectively covering it and gradually extinguishing your spark. Let it breathe, come alive and rekindle your absolute birthright to set the world on fire. Without the intense desire and emotions that constitute 'your song', every miniscule and irrelevant challenge will become an impossible, obstructive mountain, an impenetrable fog that will blind your path. A pointless journey with no route or particular destination

in mind, you will assuredly lose your way, change your direction and waste your valuable time.

2. Write it down. This is the language directly from your heart, these words are your desires and cravings, animate them with emotional attachment, the very words that will describe your feelings once your song has been successfully achieved. Then intently stare at what you've written, there is a psychological and spiritual magic in your sincere words, let them be encapsulated within your devout emotions, sinking deeply into every membrane of your body, until you are awash and drowning in their almighty power. This is your song, your life, the metaphorical book my English lecturer passionately harangued us about. These words that represent your song will set the world on fire. The visualisation of your song on paper will overpower you with an agonising, exaggerated and potent string of emotions, everything from excitable and fierce exuberance to downright agitated fright. The immensely wide spectrum of feelings is astounding, this is the exclusive power of your song, creating excitement from its potential and the fearful doubt of underachieving and living a life without 'your song' being accomplished. It was imperative for 'Motivation from a Tortured Mind' to instigate these emotions, otherwise a single word would not have been written. Entwined within every spirited, self-confident thought was a sense of sheer ambiguity and doubt, a mandatory and unavoidable requisite when attempting such magnificent feats. Such misgivings encouraged success and determination, seldom damning and clouding the conclusion of my song with impeding negativity.

3. Set a date. When will you sing your song? When will the words that mean so much, metamorphose into an invincible reality? When will that smouldering spark convert into a pyrotechnic burst, colouring and illuminating your sky? The anticipation of which will reawaken and inflame your emotions and senses on a daily basis. Without a deadline your goals are nothing more than great considerations and

great considerations alone are an exercise in outstanding futility. Mental analysis without a timeline has produced untimely, gargantuan unfinished masterpieces, ones which doubtlessly had the burning promise of setting the world on fire but will never be more than an insignificant candle in the wind, extinguishing with the most subtle of life's imminent breezes. Everything begins with the thought process, however an ending and fruition of thinking is only materialised with a specific deadline. The deadline for 'Motivation from a Tortured Mind' was rigidly set in concrete as was the vision and consequences of accomplishment at that compulsory date. Creating a resolute timetable induced an austere strategic blueprint, designed to complete the symphony within my head.

4. Draw the blueprint. This is the layout of your game plan. The precise methodology, approach, tactics, system and outline action that will perform your song within the timeframe you have decided. 'Your Song' is the beautiful destination you're infatuated with, your uncompromising timeline is set and the clock is now inflexibly ticking. No journey to any destination is possible without a map. This is the intricate details and actions that will get you there. The essence of writing a book was a gargantuan and cumbersome fifty thousand word mountain in front of me, so immense I couldn't see past it, over it or even a path leading to it, however I wholly and with a melodramatic intensity believed, with every ounce of my spirit and soul that I had to scale the un-scalable. There was no option other than to find a path over, around or through the mountain that was blocking my view. The contemplation and discipline of writing so many words was eagerly clouding my vision, shadowing my resolve and attempting to dampen the enthusiasm of my song. Despite the oppressive hindrance, my song bellowed and blared incessantly, wilfully crushing the obstacles and enabling me to concoct a cunning plan to heroically ascend the mountain and conquer the discouraging dynasty it had become in my mind.

5. Check the validity. This is the reality check of your song, your date and the blueprint. Anyone can walk on the moon, if they can find a rocket, launch it and have the expertise to navigate space. Whether a moonwalk is realistic is entirely another matter. Checking reality is a vital cog in the machinery of achieving a goal and can be summed up in one sentence 'are you committed and prepared to follow through each planned step on a daily basis, despite the calamities and obstructions that life and people will undoubtedly throw at you, within the timeframe you've allowed?' It's a level of acute awareness that has to be predetermined and calculated before you begin your fantastic journey of achievement. Intrepid mountaineers understand long before they take their first step onto Mount Everest that they will encounter numerous difficulties when attempting the climb, including the macabre remains of failed mountaineers frozen in time. Imagine the shock of stumbling over dead bodies had they not factored in such an obstacle into their reality check. If the answer to your own personal reality check question is 'no', then two menacing questions need to be addressed before you take your first step.

   a. Are you certain its 'Your Song', one that evokes exhilarating, potent, heartfelt emotions of excitement and fear?

   b. Is your timeline unrealistic, as that will dictate the amount of daily, weekly and monthly action involved to accomplish 'your song'?

Answering the first question positively is the magical cornerstone of moving forward, otherwise defeat in fulfilling goals, will be inevitable and equivalent to lighting a candle whilst it is immersed in water.

6. The final step before you embark on your intimate, fervent adventure is psychological preparation.

Be prepared. Everyday 'your song' must be played in your mind. The melody and magic of achieving your goals will be the force field that effectively and abruptly defends your beliefs from the barrage of arrows that will be shot at you.

'You write a book! You'll never do it!'

'Your book will fail. There are a million books out there. Why would anyone want to read yours?'

'I know someone who wrote a fantastic book once but no one liked it.'

'You'll just end up with a garage full of unwanted books.'

'It takes someone very special to succeed as a writer and very few writers are special.'

These are just a selection of the comments people made when I mistakenly told them about writing my book. Negative affirmations synonymous to the frozen dead bodies on Mount Everest, generally spouted by people who may have not understood the antagonistic magnitude of their flippant, indelicate and pointless ramblings. Naturally, some of these comments came from goal-orientated, educated, skilled people for whom I had a modicum of respect for, which by sheer virtue of who they are fires a sharper, fiercer arrow, far more capable of penetrating a stronghold of belief, certainly in comparison to an arrow shot by someone with a lesser hierarchy in my mind.

'Your song' is the inordinate, colossal shield that will inoculate you against the deadly, ceaseless archers and snipers. Even though some words that people have indiscriminately discharged have raised my doubts and chinked my substantial armour, the consuming emotions attached to my project ardently kept me on track. Negative people are rampant and will prevail, strategically weaved into all of our lives, that is a foregone conclusion, it's your preparation for them and the sturdy resolve of your goals that will always keep their pointed, absurdities from piercing and damaging your confidence.

Every sunrise will present glowing reasons to not fulfil your ambitions, everything from your own comfort-zone laziness to the deluge of unhelpful comments and attitudes from the people that tessellate your life. The unadulterated conviction and resolve of your goals will only be magnified, strengthened and fuelled by the very things that would assuredly annihilate goals of a weaker, less meaningful disposition.

The dark, shadowing clouds of negativity that have always emerged when I've shared my goals with certain people, sparked sharp, intrusive lightning bolts that spurned and powered my willpower to pursue my goals. 'Motivation from a Tortured Mind' followed the six step process above. This goal has illuminated and vibrated every cell of my mind and body with an irreverent fear and an uncontrollable excitement, from the very moment I realised it was my song, it established itself as a life altering epiphany. A deadline that was set in stone, it never faltered and only spurred the weekly activity, broken down into doable chunks of one thousand words every week. Through every travesty, cynicism, discouragement and obstacle the action plan remained resolute and scrupulously on track to the very last word.

A solid and unshakable, impassioned goal. Fiercely bludgeoning, with cold-blooded fury any indifference and swiftly establishing an organised, structured crystal clear habit of attainment.

Habit

'Your habits will either make you or break you. Build you or destroy you. Become you or fight you. Habits are your best friends or your worst enemies. Define them, control them, work them and success will be YOURS.'

The taste of dirty, cold metal contaminated my mouth, shivered through my body as the natural regurgitating action of my throat was about to make me choke and vomit uncontrollably. It was only the immediate flush of adrenalin inadvertently created through feeling helpless and dumbfounded, embroiled in such an unlikely, dangerous and above all desperately frightening situation that actually staved the projectile sick, from forcefully gushing out of my mouth.

Ten minutes earlier, after a productive and enjoyable day at work, wearing a pristine suit and long black trench coat, I left my office with a colleague, who in recent months had also become a friend that I sometimes socialised with and stepped out onto a distinguished and venerable London street. Now, as if I'd stepped through a miraculous nefarious doorway into the abyss, I'd been transported to a circle of violent, scummy degenerates. The first encounter in this cold, dubious place was a mammoth hulking, scarred black man, face shining like a poisonous black mamba snake, he spat out the venomous words 'who the f**k is this?' and simultaneously, clanking it past my front teeth, forced what appeared to be a gun, directly into my mouth. The bizarre stunt happened so fast, I didn't even have the timely thought process to blink, let alone step away. I was frozen and shocked, with the thought of a bullet piercing my head and splattering my brain all over my friend, not to mention ruining the deliciously colourful tie around my frigid neck. I'd never seen a real gun before, let alone reluctantly fellated one. My friend responded with an air of authority 'he's safe'. I recoiled in utter shock as the gun was violently pulled from my mouth, this time chipping the back of my teeth and painfully scraping the roof of my mouth. I was utterly speechless, a bleeding mouth, a black mamba ferociously waiting to bite, wielding a gun that was seconds from unleashing my very last second on earth. Just over ten minutes ago I was in a plush, magnanimous office building and now afraid and nervously shaking, in a decrepit pitiful dungeon in the basement of a restaurant, having just escaped the cutting scythe of the dreaded grim reaper.

My colleague had asked me to accompany him whilst he purchased narcotics. I should have known better but once again curiosity pushed, lured and beckoned me into the wrong but seemingly adventurous direction. An action precipitated by the commonly known drug addiction my colleague had and general nonchalant attitude towards drugs, particularly in certain London societies.

The den of thieves, vagabonds, junkies and dealers, was remarkably, below a very prestigious and wealthy London street. On the pavement ladies strutted in diamond encrusted shoes, whilst below ground this debased residue of humankind eagerly sold their souls, not to mention their shoes for the next fix.

The irony typifying the gold laden pavements of London was astounding. Underneath a glittering, wealthy society was this ignored, hidden underbelly of the villainous fallen relying on the support of gun toting cartels that supplied their addictive narcotic sustenance. The painfully thin veneer between the two contrasting cultures was bridged by the likes of my colleague, eagerly exchanging hundreds of pounds for a polythene bag of powdered white death. Legality aside, it was his prerogative to frazzle and destroy his brain. If that's how he chose to spend his hard earned income, then other than the law of the land, it was entirely his decision.

I knew this dark world of depravity existed, I just hadn't realised I walked above it every day and rather disturbingly I hadn't realised, in my own oblivious naivety it compromised the innocence of children. Wealthy business men, such as my friend buying their alternative mind torturing existence was acceptable and a result of the adult choices they had made, however children still in their angelic, teenage years, sat against the wall in a puff of deathly smoke, billowing from a glass pipe was beyond the realms of humanity and decency. There were business people living lives of decadent luxury purchased from the defilement and habits of children younger than their own and there I was stood in the centre of this inhumane addicted hell. This was manufactured purgatory, guarded by the hellish 'Black Mamba' who impulsively lashed out with a fierce back-handed swipe the face of a young woman that had dared to ask him for some more illegal substance. She fell to the floor like a flimsy playing card, blood pouring from her lip adding to an already scarred, tortured face. The girl had clearly not witnessed her twenties yet and looking at the exposed, bruised, violated state she was in, it was highly unlikely she would, far more likely she'd be another casualty of a corrupt world, just another face on a 'Missing' poster decorating an underground railway tunnel. I instinctively bent down to help her back to her feet, my compassion was rewarded with a bitter scowl and mouthful of bloodied spit forcibly expelled from her mouth, followed by a vitriolic, blasphemous outburst. I could still hear raucous laughter from my colleague and the armed security guard, as I shot out of the degenerate scum hole and stepped back into London civilisation. I hailed a taxi and went straight home, only then realising my clothes and face were spattered with the astringent blood and drug infused contents of the girl's spit.

The next day I reluctantly awaited the arrival of my colleague, he was almost always late for work. I had certainly anticipated a flaunting of his start time on this particular day, considering the amount of white powder he had purchased from the 'gear-shop', as he referred to it, the night before. Even in those circumstances of an exceptionally hedonistic evening, he was pushing his luck more than normal today, it was now midday and his chair was still empty with his in-tray overflowing with work.

Nevertheless, an inundated in-tray was undoubtedly the least of his problems, when has unanswered communication ever been a threat to life? Unlike the gargantuan life-threatening situation he had circumvented into his world overnight. He had overdosed on the narcotics and had been administered to hospital and was unconscious in intensive care. As for his in-tray, that continued to overflow, he was swiftly fired by a company that needed to disassociate itself from drug addiction and the objectionable headlines his melodramatic story was creating, particularly considering he was unceremoniously dumped in the doorway of a major London hospital, almost naked, severely beaten and hyperventilating from the overdose.

It took numerous weeks before he regained a grip on reality and started to address some of the consequences his addiction had led him to. During those traumatic days of convalescence I regaled him with stories of my own depressing time in hospital and how Hope, Vision and Possibility had been instrumental in curing my psychological blindness and giving me the metaphorical sight to change the future. The identical whispers of hope that I'd witnessed and experienced years ago, kept him alive mentally and pulled him through the trenches of drug and anguish related extreme angst and clinical depression. His positive attitude to rejuvenate his life meant seeking a cure to his addiction in a rehabilitation clinic, two weeks of unadulterated medicine, psychological reconstruction and strategic weaning off from the substances that had ruined his life and god-given ability to take control of an everyday, normal existence. Two weeks locked away with literally no contact from the outside world, an injurious world that dealt him an atrocious hand, one which he played with a theatrical disregard to himself, his family and his career. There was only one person in his loathsome world that he could rely on, only one person that his debilitating habit hadn't pushed away, that could be there at the rehabilitation clinic to take him back home. There I was sat waiting for him to be officially released. Above the secured entrance to the wards was a set of poignant words of irrefutable importance.

'Your habits will either make you or break you. Build you or destroy you. Become you or fight you. Habits are your best friends or your worst enemies. Define them, control them, work them and success will be YOURS.'

Habits are routines of behaviour that are repeated regularly and tend to occur subconsciously, such habitual behaviour generally goes unnoticed in people exhibiting it, basically because a person does not need to engage in self-analysis when undertaking routine tasks. The process by which new behaviours become automatic is habit formation. Anything from regularly going to the gym after work on a Monday, to instinctively smoking a cigarette after dinner is habit formation, a part of your daily routine. Old habits are generally hard to break and new habits are hard to create because the behavioural patterns we continually repeat are imprinted in our neural pathways, basically they become a part of us and the functioning of our brains.

A bad habit is a negative behaviour pattern and includes everything from procrastination and driving too fast to biting nails and fidgeting. The majority of habits are controllable and rely on will power to exercise the necessary control. This is the primary distinguishing factor between a habit and an addiction or illness.

Will power is the enforcement behind good habits that are essential to success and also bad habits that encourage failure, hence making the first part of the statement from the rehabilitation clinic *'Your habits will either make you or break you. Build you or destroy you. Become you or fight you. Habits are your best friends or your worst enemies',* absolutely paramount in understanding the importance of habits.

1. It certainly doesn't require the intelligent mind of a genius to conclude which habits help or hinder success and it can be simply summed up in a single sentence 'starting with the end in mind which of your current habits will slow down your journey and which habits do you need to acquire or even enhance to make your path to success feasible'.

2. The power of your goals ('Your Song') and inspiration to achieve them will encourage the formation of useful habits and the destruction of foreboding ones. If your overwhelming bad habit is simply procrastination then that is a clear omen that maybe 'your song' is not really 'your song'. The reluctance to shift bad habits could be the

greatest indicator of the strength and sustainability of your desired destination. Long before you address any negative habits, ask yourself the elementary question why? Why, is the habit a part of your daily routine? If driving too fast has become habitual and you are able to accept that as a conscious fact, then ask yourself why you drive so fast. Is it simply because you leave too late and therefore are always struggling to be on time? Or is your ego the culprit, wanting to be substantiated and energised by driving faster than the other drivers? Or does the need for speed plainly make you feel more powerful and in control. If the latter is the inducement to drive so fast, it may lead to a deeper analysis of yourself, what has happened in your life, or what is lacking in your life for the compensation to be derived from speeding in your car? Looking at your negative habits in this context will help you understand yourself and accumulate the will power required to change. There isn't a single habit that can't be strategically assessed and consequently controlled, weakened or disintegrated completely.

3. The key to combating negative habits is will power. The key to will power is frankly, you. The induction of that overpowering mindset begins with giving yourself powerful foundational reasons, such as your goals and the vision of what you want to become. Undoubtedly your unfavourable habits will be an antagonistic deterrent to your desires and aspirations. Don't attempt to conquer habits without the sympathetic understanding of why they've originated in the first place and how if they're not restricted or eradicated they will doubtlessly handicap your potential for success.

4. Decades ago, an esteemed Doctor concluded that on average it took twenty one days for amputees to adjust to the loss of a limb. Hence, speculating it also took twenty one days for people to adjust to any major life changes. In other words after repeating actions for an uninterrupted twenty one days, habits can be formed. There is no solid evidence of the time it takes

to firmly establish a habit and clearly it's going to depend on the type of habit you're pursuing and your passionate single-mindedness to achieve the goal. Consistency is purely based on the power of your desired result and the resilient, inspiring reasons that uphold that desire.

5. Being overweight is a consequence of habitually eating greater calories than your body is utilising, consequently the habit of surplus calories causes an increase in weight. The necessary habit of eating less or burning more calories to shed or control body weight is deemed difficult for most people because the habit of eating more is easier to do, than not to do. Particularly as the habit is imprinted in your neural pathways, it becomes a normal, natural action. The will power to counteract such an immense, accustomed habit of eating too much and exercising too little can only be successfully implemented with total visualisation of the desired effect you're trying to establish. Simply put, it's strengthening your resolve with the consistent, unbreakable desire of what you want to look like, feel like and how you want to be perceived by others, at your reduced size and weight. Another fantastic example of strategically assessing, then controlling, weakening or completely disintegrating the habit.

6. *'Define them, control them, work them and success will be YOURS'* adequately sums up the process of creating good habits that can crucially pave your road to the successes you want. Once again the formation and development of such habits wholly relies on the backbone and intensity of your goals. On a personal note it became a habit to write a minimum of one thousand words per week, whether it was rain or shine, to accomplish the almighty goal to write this book. The habit of regular writing became an intrinsic part of my weekly routine, replacing detrimental habits such as sleeping till midday at the weekend and watching excessive television, neither of which habits could have possibly stimulated and supported my passionate, heartfelt

goal. Therefore once you've established productive habits, the fruitless, impotent ones can tend to wither away to make time for the advantageous, dynamic ones that are the reinforcement and platform for your intentions.

As for my friend, the rehabilitation process to shift his habit and create a longer, healthier existence didn't precipitate, although the clinic had determined some of the root causes of his addiction and attempted to address those with positive psychology, there was an immense chasm between his desire to be intoxicated and the substantial reasons he desperately needed, to address the balance and halt the obstinate massacre of his life. Therefore in the absence of the positive counteractive habits he needed to kick his deadly habit, his negative, counter-productive habits were always going to overshadow and control his life. Which is precisely what happened, within two months of leaving the rehabilitation clinic, his life spiralled completely out of control and into utter pandemonium. Time finally ran out for him, he lost the fight and died of a massive narcotics overdose.

Tenacity

'A tenacious, forceful attitude cannot be conjured from thin air. All the facets of fear, inspiration, goals and habits will come into play, particularly in creating the very infrastructural reasons that will generate a natural tenacity to succeed.'

Every cell of her body was extinguishing its soul sustaining supply of oxygen, squeezing it out and switching the mechanism of living off. This was indeed the end of life on earth and the beginning of devoted hope. Hope that the promised-land, was more than a dark abyss of nothingness, that heaven was waiting with open arms to accept the righteous entities that gave up the fight on this mean and malevolent earth. Electrical impulses were travelling at break-neck speed, each one with a message of euthanasia, the ticking time-bomb had been detonated and General Brain was in charge of operations. *'Five minutes to termination'* he shouted enthusiastically to the millions of corpuscles that worked only under his command. *'Intensify the pain, slow the heartbeat, close the eyes, shallow the breathing'*, General Brain was ruthless and unrelenting, this was his crowning mission after decades of occupation, it was time to shut down all operations, everything was falling into place as the grand plan of death was unravelling and systems were giving up their fight to function. The metaphorical scythe was ready to swipe at the jugular and force the cessation of life. *'NO, NO, NO, NO, I want more time, I will not give you my parting breath until every member of my family has arrived'* Mum was adamant, this was her toughest battle, it would take all the intestinal fortitude, courage and sheer doggedness to stay alive for one more hour in a body that had successfully, against all the odds of disease, sickness and a callous plotting world, stayed conscious and operative for over eight decades.

The perseverance to prolong a life when the shutdown mechanisms have been detonated borders on miraculous, it would utilise every miniscule ounce of stubbornness that could be mustered. However as with anything worth pursuing that undying diligence and determination will conquer any adversity and challenge, even the fight against an obstinate brain that is scheduled to die and that's exactly what Mum did, stayed alive, keeping the grim reaper at arm's length until she was ready to meet her destiny.

A tenacious, forceful attitude cannot be conjured from thin air. All the facets of fear, inspiration, goals and habits will come into play, particularly in creating the very infrastructural reasons that will generate a natural tenacity to succeed.

Tenacity is a noteworthy bedfellow in your F.I.G.H.T, it's an inner strength and stability, unwavering and vigorous throughout all extremities. It exudes firmness in your beliefs and durability no matter how heavy the downpour, tenacity will secure your backbone and continue the battle, knowing its fuelled and anchored by the sheer force and power of your fears, inspirations and your commanding, gargantuan song.

'I'm enthralled by the concept of our capability to 'fight', against all conceived ideas and rationale, suggesting the human mind is blessed with an outstanding degree of power, arduous potential and a vigorous dynamism. Within all of us, is the desire, enterprise and driving dexterity to achieve almost anything we want to. The majority of people on this earth live unfulfilled lives, never realising or understanding their gargantuan potential and leaving their lives to the democratic guarantee and dismal certainty of one day simply becoming dust or soil, having never witnessed the cunning adequacy they had sat dormant within their own head.'

CHAPTER 10

Dreams

'*The unpredictability of our unavailing lives is inane and frivolous, with the grim reaper only ever one step behind us. Your greatest challenge is to live the life you dream of, before his deathly scythe decapitates your peripheral existence.*'

An involuntary succession of images, ideas, sensations and emotions, in various stages of sleep, dreams are not definitively understood and serve little purpose, particularly as some are threatening and confusing, nevertheless they can also be entertaining and amusing and are absolutely free, with humans being one of the few species that have this spontaneous, uncontrollable ability.

A 'lucid dream' is the definition of having a conscious perception of one's state while dreaming. In this state of dreaming, the dreamer has control over their own actions, including the characters and environment of the dream.

Our lives exist in an immense lucid dream, a world conjured through our actions and the F.I.G.H.T we're willing to have. There is no environment and situation we can't control or create, there is no part of our lucid dream that we can't improve. The tragedy of our lucid dream world is the ridiculous nature of its termination. There is no given moment, hour or day that it is timed to end. Therefore every day General Brain, Corporal

Heart and the colossal, hostile battle-field known as Earth, collaborates with our desire to live, is a gigantic blessing, knowing the futile and illusory nature of staying alive.

The precise moment we appear from the womb, an audacious plot begins to antagonise and counteract the miraculous life we're consecrated with, from that first breath of air, the forces of nature, our circumstances and the environment conceptualise our demise and endeavour to return us back to where we originated from. Every day of blessed life is a FIGHT for our right to have a place in this world.

The unpredictability of our unavailing lives is inane and frivolous, with the grim reaper only ever one step behind us. Your greatest challenge is to live the life you dream of, before his deathly scythe decapitates your peripheral existence.

Birth is a miracle, so why live a life that is short of miraculous, turn your dreams into a lucid world, one that curiosity discovers, imagination colours and 'your song' provides the everlasting soundtrack for, allowing you to blissfully dance through your limited days. Every desire you possess will illuminate the dark corridors of your mind, once your dreams are incandescently beaming in your brain. The intensity of such positive thought will radiate in all your actions. Consciously knowing with vehement clarity, infatuation and passion where you want to be and understanding how every sublime cell of your being will exude a majestic sense of achievement, will pave the way to your eminent destination.

Never relinquish your birthright to have a splendored life, glory awaits you but surrender is not an option, the grand spectacle of life does not respect or accept abdication of your dreams. Abandon your dreams and you're biting the hand that gave you the capability to rule the world. A person that reaches the heady altitude of personal satisfaction has either realised their dreams or accepted an insignificant, lacklustre existence, one in which hope alone could not herald victory, vision was only as far as the eyes could see and the possibility of their potential was impossible to imagine or materialise.

You are a literary masterpiece and yet your greatest, omnipotent chapters remain unwritten, your stories untold, your victories not testified. The glories that will enthral, enchant and hypnotize your life are all within the pen you grasp. Write your life with imagination, belief, hope, vision and possibility. Detonate your personal ticking time-bomb and light your firework, it will illuminate your world and be more grandiose than you ever anticipated. It's your story, it's your book, It's your life.